To Judy—
May the entire
and life in
millennium be
gentle to you.
Enjoy my memories.
Best wishes,
Dr. Greta Woodrow
Feb 1997
MW00416465

Memories of Tomorrow

Greta Woodrew is also the author of *On a Slide of Light.*

GRETA WOODREW

Memories of Tomorrow

A DOLPHIN BOOK
Doubleday
NEW YORK LONDON TORONTO SYDNEY

A Dolphin Book
Published by Doubleday, a division of
Bantam Doubleday Dell Publishing Group, Inc.,
666 Fifth Avenue, New York, New York 10103

Dolphin and the portrayal of two dolphins
are trademarks of Doubleday, a division of
Bantam Doubleday Dell Publishing Group, Inc.

Library of Congress Catatoging-in-Publication Data

Woodrew, Greta.
Memories of tomorrow.

"A Dolphin book."
1. Unidentified flying objects—Sightings and
encounters. I. Title.
TL789.3.W66 1988 001.9'p42 87-27182

ISBN 0-385-23887-8

Printed in the United States of America
First Edition
July 1988

BG

To our special S.T.A.R. supporters and Woodrew Updaters all over the United States, Canada, and in fourteen foreign nations who "think and relate" with us.

And . . . ever and always . . .

To E.T.I.: our fine feathered friends of the Ogatta group in the Jorpah, so near and yet so far.

To Dick: My best friend, playmate, soulmate, "relay channel" extraordinaire; my husband for over thirty-five incredible years . . . co-author, co-editor, co-lecturer, co-researcher, co-habitant. Thanks for always being there, Big D!

To my A's and J's—and their mates—for their solid support system.

To Jim Fitzgerald, Senior Editor and believer. A patient man!

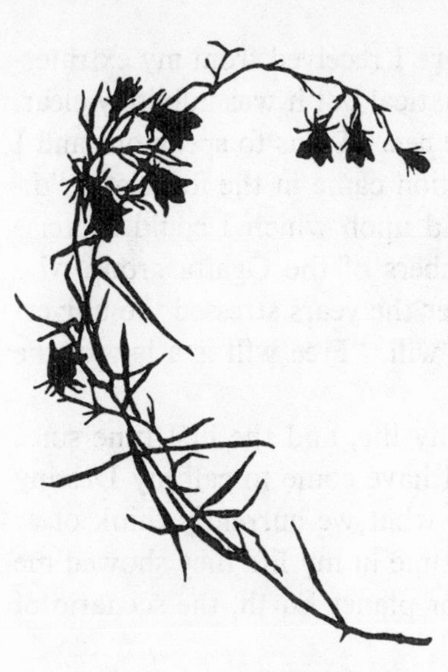

Introduction

THIS IS MY STORY. It tells how I was readied for changes by benign, highly evolved as well as technically advanced cosmic beings. "Architects of the future you must be to move into the Golden Tomorrow!" they said. "It will be a different tomorrow for future generations of human beings. And you, here and now, will need all your wits about you to survive what Man can do to Man, and Nature's Plan."

The extraterrestrials want mankind to succeed in the transitions taking place on little planet Earth. We will succeed because Man is meant to succeed. I want to share with you my memories of tomorrow—one woman's cosmic connections. As a futurist, I see my own experienced reality also as your story.

I became aware of the coming changes through the intervention of an extraterrestrial civilization, the Ogatta group. It was in the mid-seventies that they said, "Tell them. Tell them of the changes coming and of the twenty-plus civilizations who will appear in their spaceships to help humankind. Allay their ungrounded fears when they see us. You are meant to *trumpet the voice and scribe the pen about the transitions and changes on your planet."* This was the only directive I received from my extraterrestrial friends. It was not grammatical but it was infinitely clear: *"Trumpet the voice and scribe the pen."* I was to speak out and I was to write. Every other suggestion came in the form of a "direction" that I could evaluate and upon which I could exercise my free will. All seventeen members of the Ogatta group who alternately interfaced with me over the years stressed the universal importance of exercising free will. "Free will is a law of the Cosmos," they said.

Then, for the second time in my life, and the first time since my childhood, they rolled what I have come to call my Destiny Screen. It defied linear time and what we currently think of as natural law. And for the second time in my life they showed me —in living color—the *scenario* for planet Earth, the scenario of what is to come.

Hurricanes. Floods. Super-magnetic storms. Droughts. Plagues. Earthquakes. Volcanoes. Tidal waves that bury whole cities and their populations beneath a wall of water. People dying of thirst and hunger. People with burns on their bodies. Animals with hair scorched and eyes glazed. Extinction of much wildlife, furbearers, species of birds. I witnessed with horror the devastation of our beautiful planet.

But as my Destiny Screen rolled, I was told that I was looking at the survivors. And then the message came clearly: *"Despite what Man can do to Man, and Nature's Plan, there are those civilizations out there in the cosmos who believe that planet Earth is worth helping in its time of great adjustments."*

I witnessed the devastation of our planet, and it was not in the dim and distant future. It was to be in my own lifetime. In the coming decades. It had already started. And I wept for humanity. Then I began to view the Scenario in its entirety. I started to understand the signs for what they are. I can face the future more calmly, with love and faith in our ET friends. E.T.I.: ExtraTerrestrial Intelligence. These marvelous beings, with their advanced technologies, minds, and spirits, promise their aid. They will share universal knowledge with us on planet Earth. They promise to assist our entry into the New Age . . . before the turn of the century.

We live in a time of excitement and hope! It is a time for mankind to make a quantum leap forward, in consciousness and in evolution. It is a time for each of us to decide whether to be tied to a rapidly disappearing past, or to join a new and demanding (albeit a different) future. My husband and I see change taking place on every level: climatic, geological, social, economical, political, psychical, personal, familial. The Earth is being strained geologically and environmentally. New energies bombard people's consciousness. Energies that trigger stress, unhappiness, and violence in some, and expose latent psychic powers in others.

Geologists are aware that thunder precedes volcanic eruptions and other seismic activities. It happened when Mount St. Helens blew her top. On that clear day, thunder echoed for miles around. In writing this book I hope to provide "thunder" on the clear day of the present for you to read and understand. I hope you will hear it, heed it, prepare for it and do whatever you must do. So come, think and relate with me and share memories of tomorrow as we consider the New Age that is dawning.

Memories of Tomorrow

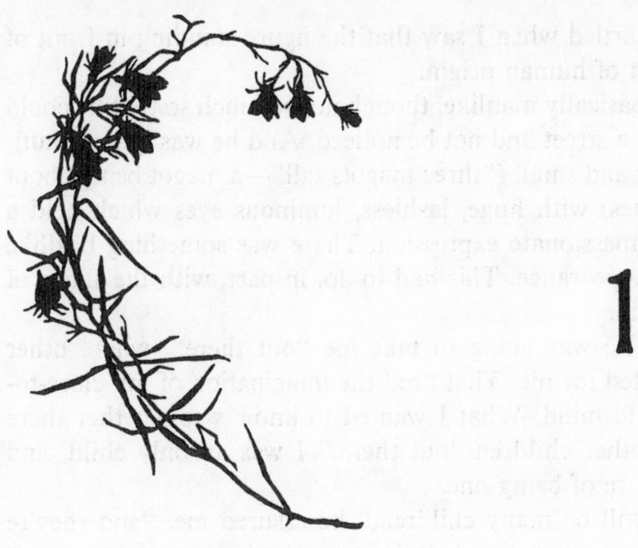

1

"CAN YOU HEAR ME?" the voice said.

The voice, rich and deep, didn't frighten me, even though I couldn't see who was speaking. It was a friendly voice.

When I heard it—an experience that would change my life forever, and in unimaginable ways—I was a three-and-a-half-year-old girl visiting her grandmother in New York City. I wasn't even supposed to be awake. My grandmother had put me to bed a few minutes earlier, but as soon as she had left the room, I promptly got up, grabbed my favorite rag doll—with a china face—and deposited myself on the nearby rocking chair. The doll and I were quietly rocking when I heard the voice and the question.

"I can hear you," I said out loud.

To this day I have no idea if the voice first spoke to me through my ears—physically; or through my mind—psychically. But there was something natural, familiar, unthreatening, about it.

The same was true when, a few moments later, out of nowhere, someone appeared in front of me. Perhaps it seems strange that I was in no way alarmed, but I wasn't. I was simply curious. I was not even startled when I saw that the figure standing in front of me was not of human origin.

He was basically manlike, though not so much so that he could walk down a street and not be noticed. And he was quite beautiful: slender and small ("three magots tall"—a magot being about fifteen inches) with huge, lashless, luminous eyes which held a deeply compassionate expression. There was something birdlike about his appearance. This had to do, in part, with the shape of his upper lip.

He said he was going to take me "out there," where other people waited for me. That fired the imagination of my close-to-four-year-old mind. What I wanted to know was whether there would be other children "out there." I was an only child, and acutely aware of being one.

"There will be many children," he assured me, "and they're going to learn what you do." That sounded pretty neat.

"Can I take my doll?" I asked.

"No," he said, "you will leave your doll and you will come back to your doll."

I was to learn that he was as good as his word.

This event, like the events that followed, was not a child's fantasy, the wish-fulfilling dreams of a little girl looking for an escape from an unhappy existence. In fact, I had always been a happy child. I had a wonderful family, and was surrounded by many relatives and friends.

I did—and do, I hope—have a good imagination. I used it frequently, but not to conjure up friends from a distant solar system. I could certainly tell the difference between the creatures of my imagination and the people (however unlikely) of the real world. And my extraterrestrial friends—as they turned out to be—were definitely of the real, if not everyday world.

Still, I learned early on not to talk about them to my parents, who would say, as they often did when I talked of something out of the ordinary, "Greta has such a vivid imagination." They said it proudly, but I knew what those words meant: that it was useless to try to communicate what I was experiencing.

The culture shapes the reality of its members, and this was the early 1930s. To step outside the norm was to invite ridicule and abuse. My parents were not sharing my experiences, which were outside any reality they could conceive of. If ever I had a closet existence, it was then.

At the same time, though, my parents understood that I had certain gifts—psychic gifts. They recognized such things because of Uncle E.A., the family patriarch.

Uncle E.A., as everybody called him, was actually my great-uncle. He was a great big man, big in body, big in spirit, big in heart. Known as "the Wolf of Wall Street," all his life he was, at any given time, either a millionaire or broke. Everything this man did, he did in a manner that was larger than life.

One thing he possessed in abundance was psychic talent. It was so powerful, so unmistakable, that no one who was exposed to it ever doubted it was there. People said he could read palms, because that was one of the means he chose to express his psychic talents. Of course, what he was doing, I believe in retrospect, was psychometrizing the hand.

(Psychometry is a talent potentially available to all of us. It is accomplished by freeing the mind so that impressions can be received. You hold the object and focus on it to the exclusion of all else. Images will start to flow when the mind is still. The trick is to state or write what the mind receives in a free-flowing way, uninhibited by the thought process. The vibrations from the object tell their own story. Unfortunately, relatively few people possess the necessary ability to free the mind of all extraneous thoughts.)

I suppose it was because of Uncle E.A.'s certainty that I shared his psychic abilities that he took me on the most memorable hike of my life. It happened just a few months before my first encounter with extraterrestrials. I have never recounted this story before, but it is important to me because it prepared me, at a very young age, for the reality of other beings and dimensions of being.

In 1912 or '13, Uncle E.A. had set up a summer camp to bring deserving but financially deprived children from the streets of

New York to the Catskill Mountains, where they could partake, for a three-week period, of some of the wonders of nature. This Camp Tranquility is still in operation.

Some twenty years later, when I was a tiny little girl three and a half years old, he asked my mother if he could take me into the woods to a beautiful, isolated spot in that camp. Of course, my mother, whose favorite uncle was E.A., said yes. She had traveled all over the world with him before I was born. I was delighted to go to the woods—or anywhere—with him.

I can still remember the polka-dot sunsuit I was wearing as he and I walked deeper and deeper into the trees. To me it seemed as if we were walking forever. Finally, however, we came to the place Uncle E.A. had in mind: a lovely clearing, where we sat down on a large, flat rock and continued our chat.

Then he said, "Gretchen"—that was his special name for me —"I want you to sit very quietly, and let's see what you can see." I sat without speaking, feeling the strength of Uncle E.A. next to me. Time passed slowly. And then, at last, we saw them.

Uncle E.A. had seated me down behind a perfect circle of little mushrooms. We were facing it when, abruptly, tiny, delicately featured, iridescent beings appeared around that circle. They danced and danced and danced. It was a lovely, moving, swooping, joyous dance. It remains so vivid in my mind that even today, more than half a century later, I can close my eyes and see it.

I was awestruck, amazed, enthralled. I watched, wide-eyed and silent, until they went away and were no more.

I turned to Uncle E.A. Tears were streaming down his face. He said, "You did see them, didn't you?"

"Oh, yes," I said.

"I thought you would," he said. "Never forget them. Wherever there's a perfect circle of mushrooms, they might appear."

I have spent the rest of my life looking for another perfect circle of mushrooms, hoping that once again I might be able to see those beautiful little beings dance, but I have never found one. When I read of the "little people" in the gardens of

Findhorn in Scotland, tears came to my eyes and I remembered that astounding outing so very long ago.

Another youthful psychic experience that was considerably less happy caused me a great deal of heartache and stress. It all began when another uncle announced with great excitement that he was going to fly to Paris. In those days aviation was a more exotic mode of transportation than it is to us today. When I was a youngster, it took twenty-six hours to make the trip on the Silver Meteor train between Florida, where I lived, and New York, where many of my relatives resided. My father owned hotels up in the Adirondacks, so business frequently took the family up north, and I made the trip—solo—fairly frequently.

Anyway, when I heard about my uncle's planned trip I became, uncharacteristically, quite hysterical. I begged my mother to call her brother, my uncle, and say, "Don't go on the plane. Something terrible is going to happen. Any other plane, but not that plane."

I carried on so relentlessly that finally my parents allowed me to make a long-distance call to my uncle. I told him I knew that he would be killed if he got on board that plane. He pooh-poohed my fears, but fortunately E.A. was this man's uncle also, and, from being around that formidable psychic, he knew enough to take heed. He agreed to change flights, to my enormous relief and to my aunt's annoyance.

My relief was sadly short-lived. When the plane went down with great loss of life, as I had known it would, I was, nonetheless, shocked and horrified. An impressionable pre-teenaged girl, I was left with a load of terrible, if utterly irrational guilt. All I could think of was, why hadn't I called the airline? Why hadn't I notified the pilot? Why hadn't I done something more than warn just this one man, a member of my family, and nobody else? Of course, to an adult the answer is obvious—nobody would have believed me and, whether I acted or did not act, the result would have been tragically the same.

2

MY COSMIC VENTURES ended totally, along with my memories of them, when I was nine years old. But in that six-year period I was given an entirely new sense of the cosmos and its occupants, the earth and its inhabitants—and myself.

I was taken Out There. That's what I called it. Out There was another place, far, far from Earth, and it was the most beautiful place I ever saw or expect to see. How I got there, at least that first time (and indeed most other times), I can no longer remember. I was just there. And I kept it to myself.

Out There, or part of it, was a village that looked nothing at all like what I knew from Miami Beach, where I was growing up. The houses looked more like gleaming igloos; they were rounded at the top, with no sharp angles anywhere. There were no doors or windows. The tops of the houses opened and shut silently, to reveal or close off the sky. And the houses had an iridescent quality. They shimmered with a rainbow of colors and were built with a mother-of-pearl-like material named "lavahn."

Everywhere there were flowers, vivid and gorgeous, with a marvelous scent permeating the air. And from somewhere, I can't remember where (if I ever knew), music was playing. It was a music I could see, just as I could hear the colors. This is difficult to describe; at the time I only wondered at it, not about it.

In my adult life I learned that our sensory ability comes from interpreting electromagnetic frequencies on sensory tuners that resemble radio bands. The specific sensation we receive from any frequency is the job of specialized sensory neurons that tell our brain what will be a sight or a sound, a taste or a smell. These receptor cells are sensitive to one class of stimulus energy only, and they define our reality.

It seems clear to me now that when I was on Ogatta I was free of the restrictions of these receptor cells and could "hear the colors" and "see the music." These remarkable sensory interpretations are part of the normal experience of the wonderful beings who live on those distant worlds. I wrote about this in the 1970s in *On a Slide of Light,* and today I smile to see Shirley MacLaine also using the phrase "hearing the colors and seeing the music." But that's good. Many have shared this awesome experience.

How can I describe the way music looks? Imagine a pulsing rainbow, a pulsing stream that you hear as you see. It was just one aspect of a dazzlingly vivid world of colors and sounds and sights denied the ordinary human eye. Wherever I went with my Ogattan friends, we were bombarded by sensations. To those in the Ogatta jorpah this was experienced reality. To me it was endless wonder.

But I was not there to be enthralled. I was there to learn, and I was there, as the Ogatta group had promised, with many other earthly children. We were never, I might add, called "children." We were called "little people." I liked that and I suspect the others did too. And in the Ogatta jorpah "big people" listened to "little people," and that was good. Little people are not bound by too much experience.

"Little people" don't relate to trauma and hardship as "big people" do. They're also not so set in their routines that change is so totally stressful. While I looked at the changes, it wasn't until I recalled these events some three decades later, as a "big person," that the horror, the suffering, the magnitude of the situation struck me fully.

We were told we had a mission. There were other missions than ours; the many who were being trained for scientific missions were taught elsewhere. Science was not going to be my job, which was just as well because it was not my interest. I, a child fascinated by the arts, was to be trained as a communicator, as were, I assume, the other children whom I saw regularly during my frequent trips Out There and to Ogatta.

Our lessons were taught inside igloo-shaped houses. Even today I do not recall all their content but I do remember well the method of teaching. It was on a screen, of sorts—it was not exactly like a movie screen. The images we saw would suddenly appear, as if out of nowhere, to illustrate dramatically the words we were hearing. We were shown many remarkable things, but the one that remains with me to this day—because I was to see it again in my adult life—was the Destiny Screen. Why were we shown it, this horrifying collage of images of destructive forces battering the Earth? "Because the time you see is the very future of your planet," the Ogattans would say.

The Destiny Screen showed hurricanes, floods, plagues, magnetic storms, droughts, earthquakes, volcanoes, tidal waves burying whole cities and their populations beneath walls of water. We saw people dying of thirst and hunger, people with burns on their bodies, animals with hair scorched and eyes glazed, whole species of wildlife going extinct. We saw a comet strike the Earth, causing massive chaos.

Then the planet settled again. There had been safe places, and there were able human beings who had survived. There were new vibrations and a new and burgeoning life. After the death, the tumult, the devastation—new life, an exciting future for mankind.

The time would come. It had started already, they told us. It was not in the dim and distant future, but in our own lifetime. I thought of my wonderful family, and I wept more for them than for the world, which to a child is a strange and almost unknown place. But when the Ogattans told me and my friends that we could take part in rebuilding a better and more wonderful world, we were comforted. Being "architects of the future" brought a sense of purpose to our adventures Out There, young as we were.

I learned that I could trust the Ogattans. I learned about their planet and I learned how to handle their vibrations, which are more energized than ours because they have had more time to mature. I was taught that we must evolve to handle higher vibrations because the Earth will be entering a new sphere where the energies are higher, more demanding. I learned to tune my body and mind so that they could come alive in a new world. I learned to hear the plants and to know the flowers around me from within; to see into the heart of a rose, to hear the beating of colors there.

Of all my childhood experiences, though, the most wonderful is of a place I think of as the "crystal forest." I was taken there physically, in one of the Ogattan ships. They call their craft "gattae" (pronounced GAT-eye). I should explain that Ogattans use ships only for special purposes—for example, if they want to take their own friendly, compatible environment with them for extended periods of time. An individual from Ogatta, however, can get from there to here instantaneously without a spaceship.

Now, in those days words such as "UFO" and "flying saucer" had not even been invented. The idea that there might be extraterrestrial civilizations was not so widely discussed as it would be in later years. The notion that such civilizations might visit us was seldom considered outside the pages of science-fiction magazines. Only in the middle years of my adult life did I hear of the eccentric writer Charles Fort, who argued, in four books published between 1919 and 1932, that reports of unusual objects in the Earth's atmosphere suggested that space visitors might be here.

I accepted my experiences—in fact I delighted in them, looked forward to them and hated coming back from Out There—but I certainly didn't discuss them with anybody.

Anyway, one night when I was seven or eight, with my parents in Florida, I walked outside in my nightgown; the Ogattans had promised they would come for me. I scanned the skies looking for one of the gattae. I had never seen one before but I had heard them speak often of the "coming of the gattae," the expression they used to describe the time they would come to Earth during our planet's period of tribulation.

So I stood there anticipating the appearance of I knew not what. And suddenly there it was: a beautiful glowing disc which pulsed and changed colors.

I don't remember how I got into it, but I remember what it looked like inside. There were about ten of my Ogattan friends inside, including Hshames and my beloved Tauri whom I had met many times before. They directed me to a chair which was much too big for me. I complained but somehow I fit into the bottom of it, if not the back, which was molded for an adult. It was deeply curved and had a mother-of-pearl look of shimmering colors.

Beyond that, I remember only that at some point during our voyage I was told that if I looked outside I would see wondrous things. A divider or something like one moved beside me, revealing a window. Outside, in what I assume was deep space, I saw what looked like lightly colored spinning balls. And always the music, that gorgeous music, was playing.

After some time passed—how could I be more specific?—we landed. When we emerged from the ship, I saw a stunning sight, a place I would later come to call the "crystal forest."

In the crystal forest the trees were very tall. At first they looked like normal, Earthly, green-leaved trees—until they started to radiate gorgeous rainbow colors. Then the trees seemed to be made of crystal. They glistened and became strangely transparent. I could see through them and inside them.

All around the trees were the same lovely flowers I had seen elsewhere on Ogatta. I was so fascinated with them that at one point I leaned forward to pick one, but was not permitted to do so.

I remember that I sat in the grass listening to the lessons that would be wiped from my conscious memory until well into my adult life.

Then it was time to go. I went back inside the ship and in due course it landed on the spacious grounds outside my house. It was early morning, just before dawn, and I recall that my feet got muddy during my walk to the house. I had to wash them before I got back into bed. My parents did not know that I had been gone.

When I was nine years old, it all ended.

I look back on those wondrous times and realize that my sensory awareness expanded remarkably in that place in the cosmos. The range of my perceptions put me into contact with what seemed to be a limitless universe. The gamut of sensations was unlimited out there, and I was in tune with the birds, the insects, the flowers, and the trees.

How else to explain it? Nature does not cease to exist where we cease to perceive her. There I was a part of her, and my so-called "normal senses" sharpened a millionfold. I could see into the heart of a flower and get into the mind of a bird. And our laughter was palpable; bursts of energy enveloped the children each time laughter rang out in that forest. It is probable—if unlikely within our restricted sensory capacities—that we saw as well as heard that laughter. Over five decades later, it resonates in my soul whenever I think about it.

To this day I do not recall the precise circumstances of the final meeting between me and my beloved friends from the Ogattan system. All I know is that they told me I would have a baby brother (as I subsequently did; his name was Sandy, and three more brothers would follow) and that I was to take care of him. He would fill a large part of my life as I grew up.

They left me with two "directions." I was to feel them in my bones rather than directly remember them, but nonetheless they would remain with me and influence me through the rest of my childhood and well into my adult life.

The first direction was "to excel." This was said in such a way that for a very young girl there was excitement and challenge in it. "You can do anything if you try" was a drumbeat my parents also put out, and it paved the way for me to develop a confidence in treading new, untried waters, unafraid. I hope the Ogatta group was pleased when in 1979, half a century later, I was awarded an honorary degree of Doctor of Laws. The citation read:

> In honoring you, the college is honoring itself, since your accomplishments are many and exceptional. You have pointed the way for women to achieve professional careers of their own, while at the same time joining with your husband in raising four brilliant and well-adjusted children. You have been a major force in compelling scientists to take another look at the nature of substance and reality. You have not been afraid to be a pioneer in the business world, in women's rights, or in inner space. As a co-founder of the non-profit foundation S.T.A.R. (Space Technology and Research), you have helped fund scientific projects in psi research. In addition, your lectures before business and education groups have enhanced your towering reputation. Truly, you are a pioneer in preparing us for the space age and for all the challenges and opportunities that lie ahead. May your name be long associated with William Penn College and with its president.

My husband and four children walked in the processional in caps and gowns with the faculty, on that wonderful day in my life. We all wept tears of joy as the president read out the citation.

The other thing that held over from my memories was a date: 1988. I was obsessed with 1988. It was part of the second direction given to me but I couldn't remember the entire direction. Something was going to happen then. There was a serious question in my mind although I couldn't remember why. In fact I still do not know why that year—this year—haunts me. But that date has stayed with me for over half a century.

In fact, just two weeks before my mother died in 1985, she asked me why I hadn't mentioned 1988 in the past few years. "You were constantly asking me back in 1935—'43—'58—'62—'70," she said. "You always asked what was supposed to happen in 1988. Then you stopped."

I couldn't answer her question then. I think I can now. I hope I am wrong.

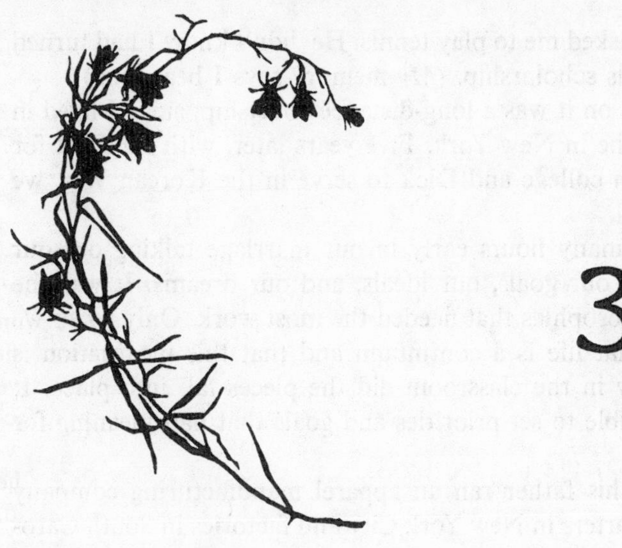

3

ONE DAY when I was fifteen years old I told my father that I was going to run for the post of secretary of the class. But my father had other ideas. To my surprise and chagrin he looked disgusted. "It wouldn't take any more effort to run for the office of president," he said.

The idea had never occurred to me. There is no greater enemy than a preconceived notion, like "Girls run for secretary" (or like the idea that my family had: that if I had extraterrestrial friends, they were the product of a vivid imagination).

I ran for president and won. I learned a valuable lesson from this: aim for the top, and never mind the hazards or ridicule.

I met my husband-to-be, Dick, when I went up to Westport, Connecticut, to visit an aunt and uncle in the summer of '47. They introduced him to me at a party. "We've been saving him for you," they whispered. I looked at him across the room, observing that this tall, handsome blond Adonis was surrounded by a bevy of females. It occurred to me that he wasn't being saved for me very thoroughly.

Later he came down the hill to the bungalow where I was

staying and asked me to play tennis. He didn't know I had turned down a tennis scholarship. *(My* memory says I beat him!)

From then on it was a long-distance courtship, since I lived in Florida and he in New York. Five years later, with time out for both to finish college and Dick to serve in the Korean War, we were married.

We spent many hours early in our marriage talking out our philosophies, our goals, our ideals, and our dreams. It was the differing philosophies that needed the most work. Only when we concluded that life is a continuum and that this incarnation is merely a day in the classroom did the pieces fall into place. It became possible to set priorities and goals that had meaning for both of us.

Dick and his father ran an apparel manufacturing company with headquarters in New York City and factories in South Carolina and Georgia. Dick and I lived in South Carolina for two years while he worked at the manufacturing facilities. I was later to run a subsidiary of the company called the Grapevine, a chain of ninety-two ready-to-wear stores throughout the South.

Our first son, Alan, was born in South Carolina, the other children in Connecticut. We had four children in five years, and it was almost like raising quadruplets. It was a big undertaking even in those days. When it came time for Dick to return to the company headquarters, we knew we did not want to raise our family in New York City. I wanted to live in Westport, Connecticut. It had a magical allure for me since Dick and I had met and become engaged there. Westport had superb public schools, which was a major consideration; also, I wanted to live near Dick's parents so that the children would have at least one set of grandparents close by. Westport was far enough from New York that it remained a small town of ten thousand at that time; and real estate was fairly priced. Although the commute for Dick was an hour and a half each way—assuming that the New Haven Railroad was running on time—he was game for it.

We built our home on seven acres and turned those acres into a landscaped fairyland over the years. For the small children, we had a tree house over a 1600-square-foot sandbox. We created a small, swimmable freshwater lake and built a Little League ball field. When the Little League period passed, we put in a tennis court and lit it for night play. We knew where our children were, as well as most of their friends!

Living next door to one's in-laws compatibly was a marvelous experience and I recommend it. When Dick's father died at age fifty-six, Dick was suddenly solely responsible for the company. He also stepped into the void to oversee his mother's affairs. He expanded the company's activities and moved into related fields. It was a gigantic task, but Dick never let it interfere with his family. We went to every play the children were in, every ball game, every recital, every speech they made. There were many such events, as all four were top students and athletes.

Dick and I spearheaded a wide variety of civic activities and philanthropies. We also saw to it that our youngsters had the opportunity to participate in many extracurricular activities such as tennis, golf, gymnastics, skiing, yoga, dancing, music, and drama. They became proficient in many and good enough to instruct in some.

As a young housewife, I became Hostess for the Fairfield Pops Music Festivals—for stars such as Rodgers and Hammerstein, Jose Iturbi, Teresa Stratas, Eartha Kitt and many others. I gave post-concert parties for stars and friends at our home, happily wearing the couturier gowns provided for each performance.

At the concerts, during intermissions, I would introduce the various stars who were in the audience, and I always made the introductions a bit different.

One night was especially memorable. As the audience came in, each member was given a book of matches and told to hold it. When the time came, I introduced each of the twenty or more big-name stars in the audience, asking each to stand up. Then I asked everyone to light a match and hold it high. And as ten thousand tiny lights flared through the concert bowl, we dedicated the light to "unity in the community."

Years later Tauri—whom I had not yet been allowed to remember at that time—said to Dick, "We were there when the channel struck light for unity in the community."

"But that was over fifteen years ago!" he said, taken aback.

"Yes," she said, a twinkle in her voice. "We've been around you for a while."

We were establishing a "credibility," although I did not consciously realize it at the time.

Education was high on our list. We financially aided twenty-two students with their college careers. Tithing was a self-imposed and satisfying way of life. High on our list of philanthropies was helping leaders—not losers.

Then came a financial catastrophe. Overnight we went from riches to rags. The hardest thing was to tell the students still in college that we were unable to finance the balance of their schooling. Three of our own children were in college at the time as well.

It took us three years to recover sufficiently to fund all prior charitable pledges, but pay them we did, honoring every pledge, totaling in the high five-figures. It was at this juncture in our lives that Dick and I recognized what true wealth really was. We watched the children rally around Dick and express their support for him and for each other. The values we had sought so long to define in our early married life were proved valid.

Meantime, Alan, our eldest, earned his B.A. and his M.B.A. at his father's alma mater, Lehigh University. Both of our daughters, Jill and Ann, had chosen formerly all-male Ivy League schools—Princeton and Dartmouth—which delighted me. "I was in the first wave that made it all possible!" I'd grin. I had been one of a group of thirty-nine women who turned the ten thousand-man University of Florida "coed" in 1947. Jonathan went to Princeton as well. Each one graduated with individual honors in various fields and sports, and that pleased me too. And each went on to climb the executive ladders in his or her own field.

Alan now heads his own land-development company in Florida, having been a marketing executive for Nestlé and then Playtex. Jill is a prominent staff writer for *Time* magazine, having been the youngest reporter on the New York *Times,* from which she went on to write for *Newsweek International.* In 1985 she received the coveted Overseas Press Award and the Page One

Award for excellence in journalism. She also edits the *Woodrew Update* newsletter. Jonathan went to IBM directly from Princeton, where he climbed the ladder from being a marketing manager with an impressive set of recognition awards, to his present post as manager of IBM's Executive Briefing Center in Endicott, New York. Ann went from Dartmouth to the American Stock Exchange in Corporate Services, becoming, in the course of a meteoric rise, the Southeast Manager of Sales. She then took five months off to walk the Appalachian Trail—solo—from Georgia to Maine, a total of 2,134 miles. Today she is Director of "Executive Reach" for Project Adventure, Inc., which trains management through an adventure approach toward organizational development.

All four are married to professionals in their own fields: an architect, two writers, and a real-estate developer. Credibility resides not only in ourselves but in our children as well.

Yet, though I did not realize it for a long time, there was another field in which I needed to establish credibility: the field of psychic phenomena and the paranormal.

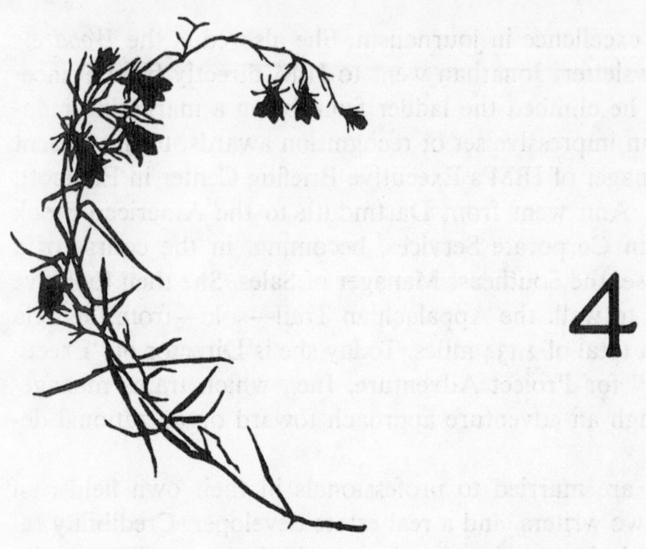

4

DICK AND I, closer than most couples, had carefully built our lives together. Still, Dick knew nothing of the Ogattans, and my own childhood memories of them lay dormant. My husband had little if any exposure to the psychic except—ever so lightly—through me. The world of business does not ordinarily encompass such things, and we were very much business-oriented. There is nothing esoteric about manufacturing apparel.

Even I, despite my childhood experiences with it, paid little attention to the paranormal. I was too busy growing up, raising our children, and—as they disappeared into colleges—establishing my own business after the Grapevine stores were phased out. It was a successful business, Executive Search, finding the right executives for the right positions in many and varied corporations. Woodrew Services, Inc. kept me hopping and productive.

I was busy, happy, content. I had not the slightest intention of changing the comfortable little world in which Dick and I lived.

And yet . . . and yet . . .

Like deja vu, vague memories would flood my consciousness

with days of my childhood when I was taken Out There, when I would see the music and hear the colors.

Actually, my reentry into the world of psychic phenomena occurred in what would appear to all as a chance encounter. But is there such a thing as a chance encounter, a coincidence? The meeting jolted me into returning to the realm of the paranormal, a realm that would lead me back into contact with the Ogatta group . . . although I had no way of knowing that at the time.

One day in August 1961 a couple who were celebrating their wedding anniversary invited us to accompany them on a night on the town. The husband's parents had flown up from Florida and were staying at the Delmonico Hotel. We agreed to stop by to see them before we went out for dinner.

When we got there, we met a woman named Mary, who turned out to be a friend of a friend, somebody the Florida couple had wanted to meet. In the course of conversation Mary told me that she was a psychic.

I wasn't much impressed. But when Mary asked for a personal item that she could "read," I reluctantly agreed, curious in spite of myself, and handed her my wristwatch. She spent the next few minutes reciting all kinds of things about my life, including things so private that they were known only to me.

I was still reeling in astonishment as she moved on from me to the rest of the people in the room. She did the same thing for them. It was an amazing performance.

Toward the end of the evening I went into the bedroom to comb my hair. Mary followed me in and gave me this message: "Your life will change very drastically in eight months. There will be a death. In the long run your life will be the most deeply affected."

Her words chilled me. When I asked her frantically if my husband or one of my children was going to die, she told me it was somebody else. I demanded to know who.

"Your father-in-law will meet an untimely death," she replied, "and your life-style will undergo the greatest change of all."

That made no sense. I loved my father-in-law deeply and I

could not imagine what she meant by saying I would be affected most of all. What about Dick—his son, his business partner?

I pleaded with Mary not to tell anyone else what she had told me. But after we left, she told our friends' parents, who called the next morning to apologize for "that ridiculous prediction Mary told us she gave you." They seemed embarrassed and I assured them that I hadn't taken any of it seriously. In reality, during the weeks and months that followed, I was practically beside myself with worry.

Sadly, the prediction came true. Eight months later, a few days before his fifty-seventh birthday, this vital, healthy man returned home from a game of golf, feeling—and looking—terrible. My mother-in-law and I immediately called a doctor, who summoned an ambulance. In the hospital my father-in-law slipped into a coma. He died three days later as streptococcus ran rampant through his body.

As these terrible events were happening, the prediction that had so occupied my mind these past eight months slipped completely from my memory. After my father-in-law's death that memory returned. For the first time I told Dick about it.

He simply could not believe it. But when other people who knew of the prediction confirmed it, he was forced to change his mind. Soon thereafter the two of us called on Mary, who remembered nothing of the prediction even after I recounted it for her. As I was doing so, it came to me that no good psychic would have burdened another person with so distressing a prediction. I still feel that way.

"How did you know?" I asked her.

In response she walked slowly over to me, took my chin in her hand and looked deeply into my eyes. I will never forget what she said next: "Why ask me? You are far more psychic than I."

That was the beginning of the fulfillment of the second part of the prophecy. From that time on, my life was going to change in ways that I could never have foreseen.

Her words ringing in my mind, I decided to find out if she was right. Like anything else, I felt, ESP was an ability that could be developed only with practice.

So I started simply, with cards. I placed them upside down and tried to separate them into reds and blacks. Even at the start I wasn't doing badly, regularly getting an impressive percentage of hits. But in time, after much practice, I would finish with two piles of twenty-six cards, one all red, one all black. Every time.

At Duke University Dr. J. B. Rhine devised a series of experiments to test a person's ESP abilities. One was a test of tactile sensing, sensing with your fingertips. He used an ordinary deck of playing cards held face down by the participant, who would then "sense" which cards were red and which were black. The participant was instructed to divide the deck into two piles without looking at them, one stack with the reds and the other with the blacks. Since red and black each emit different frequencies this is doable. Dr. Rhine invited me to Duke University several times to become part of his statistical databank in 1965. "Would you be willing to take part in some new tests we are using here which would come within the scope of what is commonly and perhaps a little loosely called psychometry? I think you would probably like them and do well on them . . ." I declined all invitations.

I began to experiment with psychometry, holding an object and picking off its recorded secrets. All the objects we wear—rings and watches, for example—store the energy bursts of the person wearing them. A sensitive person can read the information in much the same way that a computer reads a programmed disc. It is by holding objects belonging to missing persons that psychics have been so helpful to the police in locating them when all "normal" measures have failed. I soon discovered that I was pretty good at psychometry.

From there I went on to experiments in telepathy, primarily with Dick. When we were separated by long distances, we would play a series of games in which we tried to communicate simple messages or images. We took turns being sender and receiver. It worked! We communicated.

I remember one episode especially well. Dick was scheduled to fly to one of his factories, so we set up an experiment from the air. He was to be the sender. "Don't make it anything obvious," I suggested. "Keep it to four or five words and make it a phrase, not a string of objects." We established the precise ten minutes during which we would concentrate, he on sending, I on receiving.

As it turned out, I was preoccupied with other matters at the scheduled time, and I forgot all about our experiment until it was time to go to bed, many hours later. "Whoops," I thought, "poor Dick was concentrating away and I didn't even give it a try." As I sat on the edge of the bed, it occurred to me that energy can be neither created nor destroyed. "That message is still out there," I mused. "So what if a few hours have elapsed? Maybe I can still link in."

I closed my eyes, blanked my mind, and reached for the message.

But it was a strange five words that I wrote down: TALENTS ARE MANY FOR YOU. Following the system we always used, I folded the piece of paper into an envelope and sealed it. When Dick returned, his message, also sealed in an envelope, would be handed to me as I handed him mine. Ruefully I also noted on the envelope the time of the telepathic endeavor—and the hour in which I "received" it.

A few days later, after Dick got back, we opened our envelopes. His message read USE YOUR MANY TALENTS. I was enthralled with the "hit." In psychic experiments of this nature, I would soon learn, the American Society for Psychical Research evaluates a result as a hit, miss, near-hit, or near-miss. I was amused to find out that this one was judged a near-miss. *I* thought it was fantastic!

Dick had experienced one memorable manifestation of psychic phenomena prior to our marriage. Oddly enough, I was with him at that time. It was the night before he left for overseas duty with the Navy during the Korean Conflict in 1951. We had recently become engaged and I'll never forget the last night before he left. All we wanted to do was to go off somewhere alone and talk about our future. Instead we went to see my grandmother Blanche so that she could have a final chat with him. She insisted that I take Dick across the street to meet her brother, my great-uncle E.A.

Here we were, Dick in his natty naval officer's uniform, I all dressed up. The last thing we wanted to do was to waste time with relatives. But we went. When my grandmother, the adored matriarch of the family, said to do something, I always did. Dick didn't know about Uncle E.A.'s psychic abilities (or, for that matter, about anybody else's, at that time in his life).

At one point in the evening I asked my great-uncle to read Dick's palm. Dick blanched noticeably. E.A. insisted that he hadn't done that sort of thing for many years. I pressed him until he reluctantly took Dick's hand in his and searched the palm. After a glance he turned to me and remarked, "Well, we finally have a decent match in the family! You picked the right man."

Dick looked skeptical, and when E.A. noticed that, he laughed. Resuming his scrutiny of Dick's hand (though this time with a twinkle in his eye), he asked me, "Did you realize that you're marrying a deformed man?"

Dick yanked his hand away as if it had been burned. "No, sir!" he sputtered. Undaunted, Uncle E.A. said to him, "The little toe on your left foot is twisted across the next toe. It's a hammertoe. A deformity."

"Oh, that. It's congenital," Dick said, actually blushing. Then he took his shoes off because he couldn't remember on which foot the deformed toe was. Afterward he maneuvered me to the door as quickly as he could and got us both out of there. He wasn't used to psychic displays and they made him awfully nervous. To this day, however, Dick will say from time to time, "Why didn't I let your Uncle E.A. continue?" (E.A. died that summer.)

As our friends became aware of what we were doing, they urged me to undergo scientific tests at a parapsychological laboratory. The idea had a certain appeal to me because there was no one who could tell me what was happening to me or could explain it in a way that was logical to me. I also had the sense that my abilities were of some scientific value and might contribute to parapsychology's understanding of the mystery of ESP.

I approached the American Society for Psychical Research

(ASPR) and offered myself as a guinea pig. Periodically I would take the train into Manhattan and spend an evening with other guinea pigs. We participated in triple-blind experiments testing our psychometric abilities. I did quite well—too well, as it turned out. In fact, I was doing so well that the parapsychologists, who I had thought would be thrilled with my successes, were frightened. Not thrilled, mind you, but frightened!

Things came to a head one night when six of us guinea pigs were sitting together and I suddenly became aware of the presence of a seventh. I described him in detail to the rest of the group. The problem was, nobody else could see him—but somebody knew exactly about whom I was speaking. It was his grandfather, who had just died. I had never met either of them before in my life.

There was a night when I was accused of making a "disturbance." I have no memory of this. All I was told, later, was that I had gone into some altered state and begun dredging up a great deal of highly sensitive psychic information that, it seems, the parapsychologists did not want to hear.

Soon afterward I received a letter from the ASPR informing me that my services were no longer required. This was quite upsetting. I felt more alone than ever.

It was at this time that Dr. J. B. Rhine wrote urging me to come down to his laboratory at Duke University. His invitation was cordial, but I felt badly burned by the experience with the ASPR, and I turned him down.

For other reasons, too, I was growing increasingly reluctant to use my psychic powers for the sorts of "readings" people were always asking me to do back in the late sixties and early seventies.

These readings started with the past, moved to the present, and ended with the future. It slowly began to occur to me that being deadly accurate about the past and the present (both easy to validate) made the predictions of events to come ring with an authority that made me uneasy. People were inclined to accept whatever I said about the future as set in concrete, inviolable and absolute. I worried about breaching their free will and pondered the ethics of telling someone about his or her future. (There is another aspect to doing "readings." People are worried lest I read their minds. This is a needless concern. I do not read minds; I am merely sensitive to their pressing needs and concerns. I pick up the auras and electromagnetic waves that surround them, and extrapolate information from their human imprints. If, however, I find I am an unwelcome guest in the *mind* of another, I leave quietly, without poking around. I stand strongly behind the right of privacy and the need for every human being to express his own free will.)

Two incidents in particular brought everything to an end and brought my career as a working psychic to an abrupt close.

The first of them began with a telephone call. I heard a long-distance operator ask for me. Then a male voice spoke. "This is a senator in Washington. Can you help me?" it asked.

"A senator?" I said. "Do you have a name? And how did you get to me?"

The senator wouldn't answer either question. He quickly went on to tell me that his wife had lost an unusual pin, a family heirloom, originally owned by his great-grandmother. He wanted to know if I could tell him where it was.

I had never located a missing object over the phone before, but something told me to ask him if his wife did any gardening. He allowed that was true.

"Has she planted any pansies lately?"

"She has a gorgeous pansy garden," he affirmed.

"Tell her to go look near the little pansy-faces and I do believe she will find her pin lying there," I told him.

Sounding excited, the senator said he would run outside and check. He put the phone down for a short while.

Now he was so excited that I could hardly understand what he was saying. "It's here in my hand!" he shouted. "It was there where you said! This is amazing! Amazing!"

Naturally I was pleased to have been of service. And, figuring that now he owed me rather more information than he had given me at the start, I said, "Now, Senator, won't you tell me your name?"

The excitement abruptly left his voice, which now sounded horrified. "Oh, no!" he said. "I'm grateful to you, of course, but I can't afford to take the risk of having any of my constituents finding out that I consulted a psychic. You understand. It's so . . . so . . . flaky!" And so saying, he hung up.

That incident, infuriating at the time, seems amusing in retrospect. Far more sobering was one that occurred around ten forty-five one night when a man showed up at the door of our house and demanded a reading. I was tired, not really dressed or prepared for company. He was insistent.

Reluctantly I made him a cup of tea and took his watch, intending to pick up psychic signals from it. None came. I tried to force it, to no avail. It seemed hopeless. The man was watching me expectantly.

I started to watch his body language. I threw out questions and watched how he responded to them. I could tell when I had a hit by the way he reacted. It wasn't hard. Magicians call this "cold reading" and claim that all alleged psychics practice it. But I had never practiced it until now. When his eyes would light up, I'd keep going. When they'd frown, I'd move along.

After about ten minutes I just couldn't stand it anymore. I was cheating and there was no way I could rationalize it to myself. I stopped and told the man exactly what I was doing. "I just can't do this tonight," I said. "I'm not clicking. I'm overtired and, frankly, I'm just rambling based on your body English. Sorry."

He did not thank me for my honesty. Instead he said in a belligerent tone, "Young lady, do you know how far I've come?"

I thought, "Who asked you?," but resisted the temptation to say it out loud. I got him out the door as quickly as I could.

Then I went upstairs, woke up Dick, and said, "You're not going to believe this, but do you know what I just did?" I told him. "That's it for me," I declared.

And it was it, at least for my career as a "reading" psychic. It wasn't an end to my psychic ability, which was not about to be turned off so easily. Nor was my overriding curiosity about the nature of this strange gift dimmed. I still need to talk with somebody who could explain it to me.

The search took me to strange places, including séances. I look back on those years as my "Indians with tom-toms" period. All the mediums seemed to have contacts with Indians with names like Silver Birch and Bent Twig Trees. Now and then, an experience left me wondering if there were really something very real "on the other side." But more often than not, I felt that the people attending were being fleeced. And yet . . . and yet . . .

One night I went to Shelton, Connecticut, to sit with a group attending a session with a well-known medium. The place was in a remote location, and when I found it, I was very conscious of locking the car door and tucking my keys deep into my purse. Furthermore, I had stopped at the bank and knew I had a large amount of money in my wallet.

Clutching my purse to me, I went inside, and the purse never left my lap. But at the end of the session, when I went outside to get into my car, the search for my keys proved fruitless. They were gone. I flew back into the meeting room and looked everywhere to no avail. My wallet was intact but the keys were definitely gone.

A kind elderly man walked back to the car with me, and as we approached he asked what "the light" was in the front of the car. As we neared the door on the driver's side, we saw that the dashboard panel was glowing—and swinging in the parked car's ignition was my set of keys! The door was still locked and it had to be jimmied so that I could get inside.

All the way home I kept repeating, "Whoever you are, don't hurt me!" The keys glowed in the darkness of the car, yet were cool to the touch.

My heart thudded for days afterward, and I simply could not figure out what had really occurred on that strange night in Shelton. I went back there a few more times, only to become convinced that a lot of chicanery was being practiced there. I had an uncomfortable feeling that the weak, the desperate, and the vulnerable were being preyed upon. Séances were definitely not what I was looking for.

I continued my search quietly, privately. I read a good deal, but a pressing need to talk with somebody with great expertise burned inside me.

Ten years later I found that somebody.

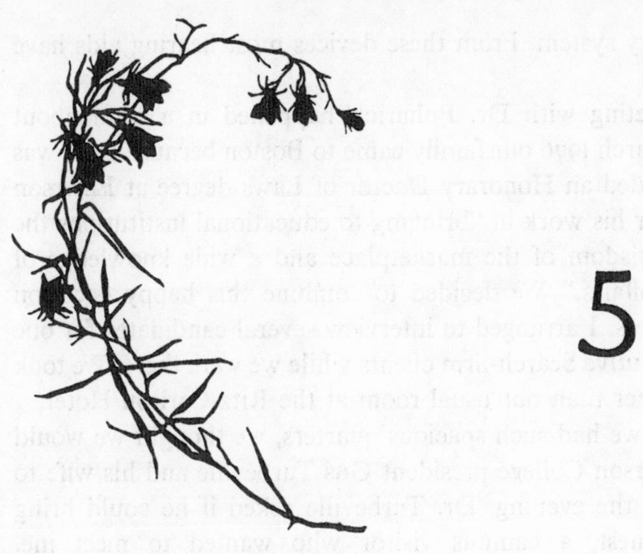

5

DICK AND I HAD HEARD, from time to time, of Dr. Andrija Puharich. We were led to read some of his books: *The Sacred Mushroom, Beyond Telepathy,* and the fascinating *Uri: A Journal of the Mystery of Uri Geller.* Puharich had met the metal-bending psychic in Tel Aviv in 1971 and spent some considerable time in his company, undergoing incredible adventures which linked Geller's paranormal abilities with extraterrestrial intelligences.

Long before that, however, Puharich had established himself first as a medical doctor (a cardiologist) and researcher before embarking full-time, in 1948, on research into the physico-chemical basis of paranormal phenomena. That year he set up his own lab for the study of ESP. In the years following, except for two periods in the 1950s as a U.S. Army physician, he devoted his energies to parapsychological work. He has studied some of the most noteworthy paranormal incidents to occur in modern times. His contributions to the field of parapsychology are legion. A versatile, multilingual man—he has often been called a genius—he holds more than fifty patents for unlocking the electrical life of the auditory system. From these devices most hearing aids have developed.

Our meeting with Dr. Puharich happened in a roundabout way. In March 1976 our family came to Boston because Dick was to be awarded an Honorary Doctor of Laws degree at Emerson College, for his work in "bringing to educational institutions the practical wisdom of the marketplace and a wide knowledge of men and affairs." We decided to combine this happy occasion with business. I arranged to interview several candidates for one of my Executive Search-firm clients while we were there. We took a suite rather than our usual room at the Ritz-Carlton Hotel.

Because we had such spacious quarters, we thought we would invite Emerson College president Gus Turbeville and his wife to join us for the evening. Dr. Turbeville asked if he could bring along a guest, a campus visitor who wanted to meet me. Turbeville, who had visited us some months earlier and seen my collection of books on ESP, was aware of my interest in psychic phenomena. He said that he had told his visitor about me, informing him that I had considerable psychic ability. The visitor expressed a desire to meet me. His name was Andrija Puharich.

That evening the Turbevilles, Dr. Puharich, and a number of trustees and faculty members from the college came to our suite. Soon Puharich and I were engaged in conversation and not long afterward he suggested that we go to one of the unoccupied rooms. When I hesitated, muttering a feeble excuse, he tactfully invited a female trustee to join us.

After we had adjourned to the room, Dr. Puharich asked me to try to "pick up some impressions" of our companion, a woman whom I barely knew, having been introduced to her earlier in the day, when we exchanged a few words of polite conversation. I asked to see her watch, and as I held it in my hand, images came quickly to my mind. I couldn't stop talking. Finally, when I began touching on some highly sensitive personal problems, the woman begged me to stop. Tears were flowing down her cheeks as she asked, "How could you know all that?" She squeezed my hand and left the room.

Impressed by this display of psychic virtuosity, Dr. Puharich assured me that this suggested I could be a good hypnotic subject. Despite my reservations, following his instructions I lay down on the bed and removed my belt and shoes. I could hear his voice softly counting . . . counting . . .

The next thing I knew, I was sitting up, no longer hypnotized, and Andrija was speaking to me in an excited voice. "My dear child," he said, "through you I have been speaking in Arabic to an old friend of mine. He was Eileen Garrett's guide and he always greeted me in a very private way known only to us both." The "old friend," according to Puharich, was an Arabian doctor who last lived in the twelfth century!

Irish-born Eileen Garrett was one of the most remarkable psychic mediums of the twentieth century, as well as an active investigator of her and others' paranormal experiences. She was the highly respected founder of the Parapsychology Foundation in New York. Andrija had worked with her in the late 1940s, when both of them were involved with a research organization called The Roundtable.

"In Arabic? Me? Impossible!" I protested.

But it was so, Andrija insisted. He wanted very much to continue working with me, he said. I was willing, but there was the problem of our schedules—we both led very active lives.

So it would not be until the next Thanksgiving, November 27, 1976, that we were able to meet. Dick and I invited Andrija to join us at our home for Thanksgiving dinner. Our four grown children were eager to meet him. They had read *Uri* and knew of Andrija's considerable reputation as an investigator of the borderland areas of human experience.

Andrija did most of the talking, largely because much of what he had to say left the rest of us speechless. He spoke of a great many things that day, reflecting his wide-ranging interests and restless curiosity. Most of his conversation, however, centered on his current project, an endeavor with—quite literally—earth-shaking implications.

He told us he was working with a group of young persons

whom he called "Space Kids." Although that designation sounded frivolous, what Andrija described was nothing flippant. These "kids," he said, were psychically sensitive individuals who were in contact with extraterrestrial intelligences. These intelligences were telling their Earthly contacts that a time of terrible destruction and turmoil awaits us in the years between now and the turn of the century.

The great changes to come will be initiated by geological upheaval, plagues, and famine which will destroy as many as forty percent of the Earth's inhabitants. Presaging all this will be an upswing in UFO sightings. The objects will be observed in places and circumstances that will establish their presence beyond any question. The UFOs—extraterrestrial spacecraft—will play a major role in the post-disaster "New Age," during which humanity will be radically transformed, from primitive Earthbound creatures to cosmic citizens.

All of us listened respectfully, if a bit incredulously. Psychic phenomena I could accept; after all, I had experienced them. But this? It was too much. And why was Andrija telling us this, all the while insisting that I could help him if I were willing to go to his laboratory in Ossining, New York? It was there, he said, that he used scientific procedures and equipment to study Space Kids. He had developed a foolproof method whereby he could pinpoint certain individuals who had the ability to return to a "parent civilization" and awaken to their "mission" on Earth. He thought I might be one of those people.

I'm afraid I laughed out loud. To my surprise, the rest of my family did not share my amusement. If they did not seem entirely ready to embrace the idea of space contacts and imminent apocalypse, at the same time they were more open-minded about these possibilities than I was. Anyway, they argued, what had I to lose by going to the laboratory? If nothing else, it would be an interesting experience. And if it proved to be pointless, I wouldn't have to pursue it. Besides, within our philosophy of a life continuum, parent civilizations seemed a distinct (if bizarre) possibility.

Reasonable arguments. As I reflected on them, I couldn't think of any way around them, whatever my reservations. Besides,

Dick and the children weren't letting up. They really wanted me to go. Their curiosity had been aroused and, as I was beginning to realize, so had mine. The next morning I told them I would do it.

6

A DAY AFTER MY BIRTHDAY, at 5:30 P.M. on December 17, 1976, Dick and I arrived at Puharich's compound—three buildings set on beautifully landscaped property—in Ossining. I, who do not believe in being sick and do not have as much as an aspirin in my house, was suffering from a massive head cold. I felt generally miserable, not only because the cold was having a dreary effect on my physiology, but also because I feared my physical condition would affect my psychic performance.

We drove up to a large frame house that looked as if it could be the main house of an old estate. We met Andrija at the door and entered the place, which I was distressed to find was quite cold. He apologized, explaining that a lighting fixture had just short-circuited and he had had to open the windows to clear the house of the acrid smell.

I told him I was afraid all this, along with my cold, was going to make me less than a perfect subject, but Andrija seemed unconcerned. He asked me to pick up any impressions that came to mind. I mentioned a few and most were direct hits. Two that weren't had to do with a couple of odd names, Astri and Shaymz, that made no sense to anybody.

Andrija led us out of the living room and through the dining room, at the far side of which was a door leading to his "work room." It was his Faraday Cage, a room encased in copper (in fact it looked something like a copper meat locker) so that no sound or object or electrical interference could penetrate the thick walls. It was loaded with recording, electronic, and other scientific equipment.

After a quick excursion there, we followed Andrija to his second-floor bedroom, which also turned out to be a well-stocked working room. Half of it was consumed by a king-sized bed, with recording equipment off to one side. The other half had floor-to-ceiling bookshelves and a raised desk.

"Where would you prefer to work?" Andrija asked politely.

"This room has a good feeling to it," I said. "Let's stay here."

Andrija disconnected the telephone to the room and set up his recording equipment as I lay down on the bed and tried to relax. Dick settled himself down near the foot of the bed, tape recorder in hand. Then Andrija put me into a hypnotic state. Things started happening immediately.

The first was a burst of starlike dots blanketing the ceiling. These were visible to Andrija and me but not, for some reason, to Dick, who was carefully monitoring the session. The impression I had was of a comet consisting of millions of tiny gold stars, with shimmering clusters that were especially bright on the right side.

I also had the feeling that I was floating, as if a part of me had left my body, and I had no sense of time. I was having an out-of-body experience. I was about to project myself astrally . . . somewhere . . .

"Are you getting any impressions?" I heard Andrija ask.

Indeed I was. "A man who's wearing silver, all over. Like a costume," I replied. "I see a birdlike creature in a silver outfit . . .

"A long dark tunnel—and a manlike creature standing there! He's got a birdlike face with human eyes. His upper lip is part of the birdlike beak but the lower lip is more like ours. He's tall, has legs with boots on, not bird legs. He's dressed in a silver-lame type of outfit. Marvelous eyes, golden, human, marvelous eyes. I see two others exactly like the first one."

One of them was "speaking" to me but his lips weren't moving. But I could hear his "words" in my mind. He was telling me his name was "Shaymz." He and his companions were from "Ogatta."

"Does that ring a bell?" I asked Andrija.

He said, "That's a new one to me." He urged me to go through the tunnel. I tried but I couldn't.

"The birdlike creatures are in the tunnel," I told him. "They're just standing there, almost like they're guarding it. I can't seem to get through . . . I see a structure, like Stonehenge."

Andrija wanted me to go inside. I went around it several times but couldn't find an opening.

All of this was happening as I—my physical body, that is—lay on a bed in a darkened room, the only light emanating from a luminated digital dial on the clock beside the bed. I was fully conscious, aware of all that I was saying.

Suddenly Andrija and Dick saw me sigh deeply, then go silent. A few moments later a peculiar basso male voice, sounding like what might come from a record being played too slowly, spoke through me to deliver this cryptic message: *"Energy level low on the bed."* Then, in my own voice, I asked, "Do you hear a child crying?"

Andrija acknowledged that there was one out in the hallway and he apologized for the disturbance. "That may be enough for tonight, with your cold," he added. And he brought me out of the hypnotic state.

It was seven twelve. I had been under exactly sixty-four minutes.

Andrija replayed the part of the tape with the message. I was astounded.

"This is the first time I've ever heard a voice come through me," I said. "My God, I couldn't possibly get a sound like that through my body consciously."

Andrija explained that the message probably had something to do with my physical condition. "The cold reduced the energy level you were able to bring to the task," he said. Still, he was impressed. "We have to find out what your job is and what work you are meant to do. The next time we get together should be for three or four days, so that we can work concentratedly."

We agreed that the best time for all of us to block out that number of days in a row was the week between Christmas and New Year's. We set the time for our next meeting for the afternoon of Tuesday, December 28.

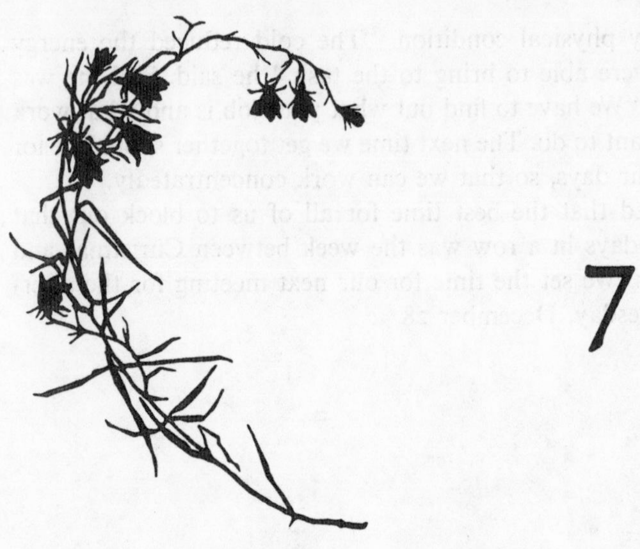

7

TWO WEEKS LATER we were back at Lab Nine, Andrija's name for his Ossining complex. My cold gone, I was highly charged, eager to begin, and curious to see what would happen. This time we were taken to the copper room and I made myself comfortable as Andrija locked the doors and prepared the monitoring equipment. I didn't have long to wait.

Hshames returned—this time he spelled his name and specified another spelling: "Astri" was spelled "Astrae," a minor planet that the "Good Doctor" (as Hshames called Puharich) should investigate via the "Berlin maps." Vesta, another name I heard, turned out to be, we later learned, another small planet of the estimated forty thousand planetoids in the asteroid belt between Mars and Jupiter.

This was all preliminary stuff, however. Soon I was gazing into Hshames's face, into his gold-flecked, huge, shining, compassionate, lashless but human eyes. Dick and Andrija could not see him but they could hear his voice, which I couldn't, as it spoke through me. He stood slightly under my five-foot, seven-inch height. Again we communicated telepathically. And again I was unable to get through the tunnel.

I finally got through it the third time around. And when I did, I came to a place where everybody knew me. They even had a name for me: "Plura." Smiling faces, small arms reaching up toward me, little hands stroking me—all this made me instantly welcome. "Plura!" reverberated all around me, and I was filled with immense joy. Huge eyes looked into my own and in their reflection I could see . . . me? I wanted to sing, to shout, to rejoice. I had come home to Ogatta.

Later Andrija spoke with an entity named Ogatta, who was named after the planet (not the other way around). Andrija wanted to know why I was called Plura.

"Greta is on your planet as woman," Ogatta said, "but an atom can split from itself. Here she is Plura. As you call it . . . a fission. She does her jobs at two levels of simultaneous existence. As the atom divides itself, so can divide the personality. Do you understand that completely? It is important that all of you do. Souls can go to more than one planet at a time. Is that clear to you?"

Ogatta said I had a "mission" to accomplish. He added that soon we would be speaking with Tauri who, although she was from the planet Ogatta, was at the moment on Vesta, an asteroid in our own solar system. She was there with Hshames, a resident of Mennon, another planet in the Ogatta system. (In the days, weeks, months, and years that followed, I was to meet many other Ogattans, Mennonites, Oshanians, Archans and Tchauvians. Sometimes we would just talk but sometimes—the times I loved best—they would take me away to that wonderful place that I recognized, somehow, as my "home.")

I was on Earth, Ogatta went on, speaking to Andrija, because I "chose to come. She knew she had to establish a strong credibility through her family—husband and children—and through her work. The first three steps are behind her. The fourth stage was to return here, which she has done, thanks to you. And now, we come to the crux of the matter. There is a coming in these decades and she has a job to do. Will she trumpet the voice and move the pen as she must do? That is the question. That is the job . . .

"There is a gathering together from many civilizations who will help your planet Earth. They will come in craft we call the gattae. The way station is on Vesta and you will hear more about that at another time. This child is to speak out on the coming of the gattae. She knows her mission."

Some of the communications that occurred during those days at Lab Nine—none of which I was consciously aware as it was occurring, and none of which I remembered afterward—were of a highly technical nature, as Andrija asked scientific questions of the Ogattans and got answers employing a vocabulary that is not my own. I did very well at college but science was not one of my interests. I took the required courses, and no more. But here "I" was talking like someone with an advanced degree in physics!

Later, Tauri came through. She was, and is, a delightful individual who manifests as a female youngster but who, as Ogatta had told us, is a highly evolved and wise being. When she came through and talked with Andrija, she spoke of me, referring to what she knew were my reservations about involving myself in the Ogattan "mission."

"She doesn't really want to write and speak out down there. She wants her privacy. She is afraid the world will move in on her and her husband . . . It's not herself that she worries about; it's family.

"When she starts to speak out, she will know those years of raising the family and building her marriage will give her all of the credibility she really needs. She doesn't see it yet. Her magnificent family connections will aid her in telling her cosmic connections! Same to be said for her business acumen . . .

"When the time is right, we will appear. More than twenty civilizations will be represented. The gattae will start to appear very soon. To small groups. No 'press,' as you call it, will come of it. Then more and more will be seen but they will not land on your ground for a while. In the coming decades the people on your planet will be prepared for the vibrations of the landings. In your time frame, much of the activity will be in the next two hundred moons [through 1993] . . . A moon is almost the same as what you call a month."

Tauri said she was on Vesta—an "ugly old place"—with her brothers Djemion and Lexitron. She was "making loops," she told Andrija; these were "energy stones to power the gattae into your dimension."

As she said these words, Andrija and Dick noticed that I was rubbing my hands vigorously together. From this was coming a noise that Dick in his notes wrote resembled a "hard rubbing sound like stones rubbing."

She added, "Do you want to see a loop? We make a lot of them, you know."

"I would like to see one very much!" Andrija replied. "Are you smart enough to show me one?"

"Ogatta says I can take one. I can take—I can—"

I slowly raised my hand into the air, palm upward. Suddenly, in full view of Dick and Andrija, a strangely colored stone the size of a lima bean materialized on my fingertips.

With Tauri's permission Andrija took the stone and examined it carefully. "Tell me," he said, "what do you do with it?"

"Why, you rub it and rub it," Tauri replied cheerfully, "and then there are two, and that is all there is to it, once you have that kind of first one. I can make them, you know."

Andrija could not recover from his astonishment. "It is technically impossible for any object to penetrate these specially constructed copper walls. Incredible the way you got it into this cage! Incredible!"

Tauri laughed about Andrija's "womb of copper."

"Would Ogatta mind if I had this stone analyzed in one of our laboratories far away?" Andrija asked.

Tauri said, "You can do anything you want to do with it. The results may surprise you!" (Subsequent laboratory analysis concluded the stone was "not of any known origin.")

"What can we do for you?"

"Help my channel to do what she is supposed to do for your planet before the coming of the gattae. *Prepare her to trumpet the voice and scribe the pen* . . . We will be there to help her once she can link into it with us . . . One by one we will make ourselves known to her."

Dick would be my "relay channel . . . and he will be the scribe and keep the records for the future references. Dick will be her dear 'Ezra'—yes! Like your 'Ezra.' I like games! I like analogies. I use analogies." (Ezra figures prominently in the Old Testament, where he is referred to as "Ezra the Scribe," one of the great reformers of law.)

Andrija wanted to know more about the Ogattans. Who was their ruler? Ogatta, Tauri said. He ruled the planets Ogatta, Mennon, Tchauvi, Archa and Oshan. He ruled as *"an entity, not a deity.* We all report to the Supreme Energy . . . to the highest order." This was made infinitely clear, repeated, and reinforced soundly.

Later we were to learn that the five planets were in the Ogattan jorpah—solar system—and they orbited on a plane or ecliptic between two stars. (Earthly astronomers would describe this as a "binary system.") The stars resided in another galaxy, not our own Milky Way, which they described only by location on the Messier List. It wasn't until several days later that I realized that the name they had for their galaxy would not be the name we might know it by, if indeed it is one of the named or numbered galaxies that our astronomers currently observe. The five planets were described as being more massive than the Earth but less dense—bigger in volume but lighter, as Jupiter and Saturn are in relation to Earth.

Soon afterward Tauri left and I returned to normal consciousness. As soon as I was able to converse, Andrija asked me where I ("Greta") had been while Tauri was occupying my body.

"I sort of zoomed Out There!" I exclaimed. "It was so real! At the risk of sounding like a dingbat, I think it was another planet."

The planet was Ogatta. Seen from space, I told Andrija and Dick, it looked like a "disc . . . covered with halves of gorgeously iridescent marbles . . . Like opals gleaming . . . colored dots."

While there I found myself in an Ogattan body. I was four feet tall and my body was covered with tiny, golden, velvet-looking feathers instead of skin. All around me everything was shining. Light covered everything.

While on Ogatta the planet, I met Ogatta the being. I told Andrija, "He has got the most exquisite eyes I ever saw or dreamed of seeing. Speckled eyes with such humanness and compassion and . . . well . . . *knowing* in them!"

Ogatta, who like all his fellows communicated telepathically, told me that I had to go back to Earth to pursue "studies." While this was happening, I would be under his protection and I could always count on the support of Dick and my children, who would be behind me all the way.

That initial meeting with Ogatta gave me a good feeling and the knowledge that I was dealing with an "advanced civilization." After all, only in advanced, more highly evolved civilizations can the citizenry afford not to mask their thoughts in language, and open their mental processes telepathically for one and all to know.

Solzhenitsyn wrote in his Nobel Prize speech: "Not everything has a name. Some things lead us into the realm beyond words . . . It is like that small mirror in the fairy tales—you glance in it and what you see is not yourself; for an instant you glimpse the Inaccessible, where no horse or magic carpet can take you." I feel that same kind of transporting magic whenever one of the Ogatta group visits or takes me Out There. It is difficult to share that Inaccessible with others.

8

WHEN WE RETURNED HOME from our incredible adventures in Lab Nine, our heads were swirling. We had been exposed to a way of life beyond imagining.

First of all, "channeling" was not a phenomenon—or even a word—with which we were familiar. I first heard it from Andrija after I returned from the altered state I had been in as he talked with Abdul, the twelfth-century Arab physician. But now I knew, from firsthand experience, what a channel is: a human being through whom things happen and information is transmitted in an awakened or a sleeping state; a human being whose body is used by other beings for the purpose of disseminating information. And I was one.

Since then I have come to think of channeling as somewhat akin to letting someone else drive your automobile as you slide over to the passenger side. If the vehicle functions properly, the performance of the car will be governed by the skills of the driver: high performance, average, poor. The vehicle is the body, the driver the life force. The driver is able to step out of his car—or slide over into the passenger seat—when he chooses. This is what being a channel is: getting out of the vehicle (body) and letting another driver (life force) in, or sharing the body with another life force (soul). This is a difficult concept to grasp—difficult but not occult.

You see, you are not "your body." Many can vacate their vehicle in one manner or another and allow another life force in to communicate. Some move their life forces aside but remain in the body. Regardless of the method used, the body functions as a machine to bring in information from another source.

This is something, that I have grown so used to that it seems utterly unextraordinary to me, part and parcel of my almost-daily existence and experienced reality.

But at that point it was all new, astonishing and not a little unsettling. And it was something we had to tell our children about in a way that made sense to all of us. As it turned out, Tauri took things in hand.

One day during a holiday break, my children Alan and Ann, and Dick and I, sat down and began to read the notes and transcripts of the tapes from my session with Puharich.

As I was reading the part about the children's role in my mission, I seemed to nod off. Then—according to my family, since I have no memory of any of this—my body started to twist and contort and my mouth tried to form words. And then Tauri came through.

She motioned to Ann to come closer. Dick wanted the children to get acquainted with her, so he asked her some questions about Ann. To that Tauri said, "Her name is Maya. She's on Vesta. I play with her sometimes. She's my friend." She was talking about Ann, who in that strange split-atom way had, like me, two existences, one as Earthperson, the other as an Oshanian.

To Alan she said, in her cheerful, almost flirtatious way, "You're pretty. You look like Lexitron."

"Am I also on Vesta?" Alan asked eagerly.

"No, you're only on Earth. You're pretty. I'd better go!"

With that I resumed reading the manuscript, as if nothing had interrupted me. As far as I knew, nothing had. I didn't find out about it until sometime later that evening, when Dick told me.

A few days later Dick and his business partner decided to take a business trip to California. They asked us, the wives, if we wanted to go with them, and of course we were enthusiastic.

I wrapped up as many of my current business affairs as I could and took the rest of them with me.

We left New York City the evening of January 10 and flew straight on to Los Angeles, where we stayed until the fifteenth, when we flew up to San Francisco.

We wanted to look up Dick's cousin Bob, so we checked into the Greater San Francisco phone book, expecting to find his listing there. But it wasn't. (We found out later that he lived about sixty miles away, too far from the area to be included.) We just about resigned ourselves to not seeing him.

So we went off with our companions to a restaurant. Dick was parking the car in a garage near the place when all of a sudden he heard someone call his name. He looked up—and there was Bob! It was a million-to-one coincidence. Or so we thought.

On Wednesday we left for Lake Tahoe, where we planned to do a little gambling before going back to Los Angeles to finish up our responsibilities there. Just before we went out to lunch, Dick took four silver dollars and put them in the top drawer. When we returned, less than an hour later, there were only three dollars. Naturally he assumed I had taken one, but I hadn't. I hadn't even seen them.

That night at the casino Dick won over one hundred dollars. As he was cashing in his chips, he noticed that he had only one dollar bill in his wallet. He made a mental note to save it because we were leaving the next morning and the dollar would be needed to tip the bellboy. But then, when we got back to our room and Dick checked his money just before dropping his wallet into the top drawer, he was startled to discover that the dollar was missing. He was perplexed and agitated, but I assured him that there had to be a rational explanation.

Having said that, I lay down on the bed and Tauri proceeded to speak, in a mock-petulant, whispery tone:

"I got your stupid old cousin and that made you happy, did it?

Well, since I can't play games with those bones [dice], I can play others. Look in Greta's wallet in front of the pieces of paper. So much for 'coincidence.' Ask her before you look, what she has in *her* wallet in singles and silver dollars, okay? Some cosmic proof for the two of you of what can be done!"

When I opened my eyes, oblivious to the words that had just passed from my lips, Dick asked if I had any singles or silver dollars. "Two of each," I replied.

There wasn't any doubt about it. I had seen the bills when I put the money—all in tens—that I had won at the casino behind them. The silver coins I planned to save.

But Dick wanted me to show him, so I obligingly opened my wallet—and there, somehow, were Dick's single and his silver dollar.

Back in Los Angeles Tauri had another message for us, as if to assure us that, underneath all her playfulness, she was communicating serious matters.

"Never mind the flip form that I take from time to time," she said. "She is a channel and you, dear Dick, take the messages as they are given. Do not ever be fearful; and scribe them down."

Suddenly the room was filled with a lilac-like aroma, a scent we would come to associate with our Ogattan friends at their sweetest. Firna, they call it. Firna . . .

This was a period of great game playing by Tauri and others of the Ogatta group. But it was game playing with a purpose. They had reopened the wonderment of the cosmos to me, and exposed techniques of the future to Dick and the children. They engaged in bits and pieces of technologies of the future that would help to make that "Golden Tomorrow" a reality. And they did it with a goal in mind. They wanted me to commit to being a channel for the Ogatta group. They wanted Dick to be a "relay channel," boosting my energies. And they wanted the children to act as a support system for me and for their activities. They knew that without the family's support I would not commit.

They went about winning each member of the family over in the manner we would subsequently learn was their trademark, "keeping it light." Laughter is a high-energy event, and the games they employed proved to all of us that *Yes!* they really existed. The activities were mind-boggling and done with great love and delicious humor. "Now you see it, now you don't" is an attention-getter when it involves dematerializing a grand piano!

My daughter Jill met Tauri for the first time late on the evening of February 4. I was listening to the tapes when I "nodded off." Jill was there to see this happen. Dick got there quickly to record Tauri's comments, some of which were directed to Jill. Jill had complained earlier in the evening that she was the only one of the four children who had not yet met the Ogattans, even though she wanted to do whatever she could for them. Tauri told her that she could help in their mission "if you want to." As Tauri said this, she looked directly into Jill's eyes, which filled with tears. In time Jill was to receive more "direction" than her siblings.

The next time we heard from Tauri was on the twelfth, when I "nodded off" during a conversation with Dick about the Ogattans and our role in their coming. As usual Dick took notes, this time on a gin rummy scorepad. He recorded six pages of notes before I was myself again.

Afterward Dick went out into the kitchen to get me a glass of water (I'm frequently quite thirsty after a channeling session). I was paying no attention to the note pad; in fact, at that point I didn't even know Dick had written his notes inside it. So I was a bit shocked when Dick came back, picked up the pad and exclaimed that the notes (along with the evening's gin rummy score) were gone. Nobody but me could have touched them, and I most assuredly had not.

Two evenings later, around eleven thirty, Dick and I had crawled into bed and turned the lights out. Dick was almost ready to fall asleep when he sensed from my actions that Tauri was arriving. He turned the light back on just as she began speaking.

"Is it all right if I use the tape machine?" Dick asked her.

"If you do," Tauri retorted, "I'll blow up the machine!" She said she had done the same thing with the notes a couple of nights earlier.

After some persuasion on Dick's part she relented. The tape ran during the entire session except for the beginning, when she and Dick had argued about the taping. Even so, several times during the ensuing conversation Tauri talked about "blowing up the machine."

After she left and I returned to normal consciousness, Dick and I listened to the tape three times and thoroughly digested its contents. We then went to sleep.

When we awoke the next morning, the tape was gone.

The following evening Dick and I went to bed and just as he was about to doze off, something hit him on the head. It was the cassette tape! At that moment Tauri proceeded to speak.

"You have a beautiful mind," she said, "but if you depend on machines and depend on the pen, then you don't think and you don't listen . . . This is not good.

"In order to sharpen your own mind, you can't always depend on a machine and a pencil, because you really don't hear. You have to listen!"

Later we were to discover that the tape was intact except for a short section in the middle which the Ogattans had, quite incredibly but most effectively, removed.

Tauri went on to say that she would blow up the tapes if Dick did not listen carefully as she spoke. "Just use the tapes later to freshen your memory," she said.

Dick said he wished he could see Tauri.

"Look deep into the eyes of the channel and one day you will see me in there," she said. "Maybe not now, but one day."

Dick looked into my eyes and replied, "I cannot see you but I know you are pretty. I know how much I like you."

"Thank you. It's nice to be liked."

Dick's—and the children's—conversations with Tauri were always easygoing. Tauri had a warmth and a humor that made her immediately appealing to all those who dealt with her. Even when she spoke seriously, there was a tender, teasing quality to her voice. All of us were entirely taken with her.

On February 21 we were back at Lab Nine, where Tauri spoke with Dick about where the future would take us. She told him:

"You may not believe me now, but your business will become secondary to this work. What you will do is vital. Her business will suffer a bit; that is the way it should be. She can cut back in the number of her clients and still have a good company. The Ogatta group will be taking her out of her body more and more often now that she has agreed to cooperate.

"As an astronaut has a 'life-support system' when he goes out in space, you, dear Dick, will act as umbilicus to Greta as she goes forth in the work. She calls you her 'power pack.' Have we not talked about that before? A prime force for energy is love. You will protect her vehicle—her body—and she can soar with confidence."

Tauri was right. Without Dick's support system I am not certain that I would have proceeded as confidently as I did. He was and is always there, a loving, calm presence. Frankly, I don't know how others go it alone. This can be very, very lonely work, fraught with unknown problems and hazards.

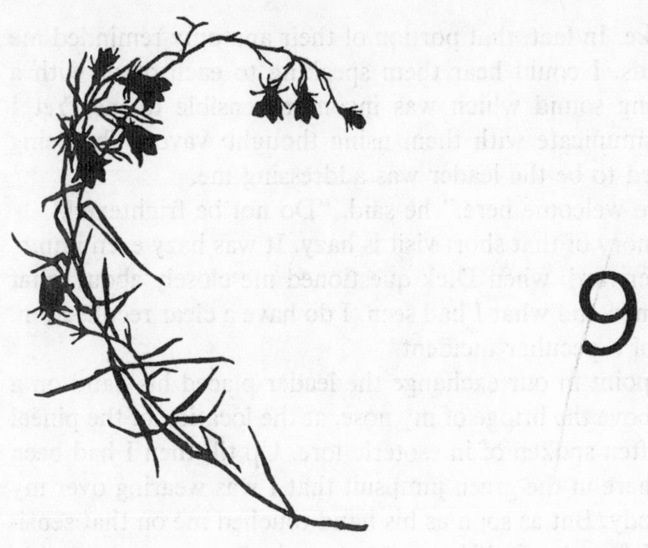

9

ONE EVENING, I had an experience with extraterrestrials who were not Ogattans. It came about as Dick and I were driving south on I-91 between Springfield, Massachusetts, and Hartford, Connecticut, returning from a two-day skiing trip to Stratton Mountain.

But on our return home, I happened to look out the window of the car, and I spotted some flashing lights. I asked Dick if he could see them. He could. Then the lights, originally on the right side of the car, swung over to the left and moved away from us.

They didn't look like lights from an airplane. We both wondered if we had seen a spaceship. To check that possibility, Dick suggested that I try to contact its occupants via telepathy.

I closed my eyes and thought, "If that's a spaceship and I'm to contact it telepathically, then I'm calm, I'm ready, and I'm willing. If that's what you really are, come back and let me see you." Suddenly it was apparent even to Dick that I was moving on to "another plane." I felt myself leaving my body.

I found myself in a room with seven or eight decidedly strange-looking beings. Their bodies were scaly and their bottom halves were fishlike. In fact, that portion of their anatomy reminded me of mermaids. I could hear them speaking to each other with a low gurgling sound which was incomprehensible to me. Yet I could communicate with them using thought waves. The being who seemed to be the leader was addressing me.

"You are welcome here," he said. "Do not be frightened."

My memory of that short visit is hazy. It was hazy even immediately afterward, when Dick questioned me closely about what had happened and what I had seen. I do have a clear recollection, however, of a peculiar incident.

At one point in our exchange the leader placed his hand on a spot just above the bridge of my nose, at the location of the pineal gland so often spoken of in esoteric lore. Up till then I had been standing there in the green jumpsuit that I was wearing over my physical body. But as soon as his hand touched me on that sensitive spot, I found myself in my Ogattan body.

As this was going on, my physical body sat slumped in the car. The only sound emanating from my mouth was an occasional gurgling. Dick tried to speak with whoever was making the gurgle. It appeared to respond, but he was unable to understand what was being said to him. The exchange ended and there was nothing but silence until I returned.

After I came back, I could still see the spaceship through the window on the passenger side of the car. I watched it for a few minutes until it disappeared.

Naturally Dick was intensely interested in what I had experienced during my departure from the body. We talked about this for a while, referring to the ship as "one of the gattae," since we were being trained for the "coming of the gattae." Then the conversation lapsed and Dick's full attention was focussed again on his driving. But only for a few moments, because all of a sudden Tauri spoke.

She said, "That wasn't a 'gattae.' Gattae are only from Ogatta, Mennon, Tchauvi, Oshan, and Archa."

"I thought that all spacecraft were called gattae," Dick said.

"Only those from our planets."

"What is this ship called?"

"I don't know. If they didn't tell you, I don't know."

Tauri later told us that a "Jack Mooney from Jericho" had seen the craft I boarded. She said he had called a local newspaper to report it but had been rebuffed. Dick took this to mean Jericho, Long Island, and offered to call the man, figuring that it would be an independent confirmation of the sighting.

"Forget it," Tauri replied. "It's too premature. We'll tell you when."

Another interesting—amusing, actually—experience occurred on one other occasion as Dick and I were traveling on the highway. This time we were on our way to New Hampshire.

At one point Tauri entered the channel and initiated a lively conversation with Dick.

"In the beginning when I'd visit," she said, "I'd say, 'I got here!' and you'd laugh and wonder what kind of 'cosmic showbiz' would happen now. Well, it was very important that we play the games for you, because interspersed in the funnies were bits and pieces of serious things that did come to pass. It was an easy way to prepare you for the real work of the future. All things tie together."

Dick asked, "Can you do something, Tauri, that ties in to nothing—just to 'bobble my mind,' as you call it? We used to have such a good time when you defied our natural laws."

"Ohhh, my goodness. You want fun and games, do you, my dear Dick? Well. Look up in the sky. What do you see?"

"Nothing. I don't see anything."

"No clouds at all?"

"No. No clouds. Nothing."

"Look again. But be careful as you drive your wondrous machine. Look straight ahead."

Tauri moved my hand slowly across the windshield.

"Good grief!" Dick exclaimed. Stretching across the expanse of sky were huge block letters spelling out the word O-G-A-T-T-A. The letters looked as if they were made of clouds.

"Can anyone else see it?" he wanted to know.

"Yes," said Tauri, "and they'll think, 'Oh, that looks just like letters in the sky!' Now look again, for they will go away quickly, quickly."

They did.

"Tauri, you're too much!" Dick said.

Sometime earlier, Tauri had provided us with another sky demonstration. When it happened, we were with a group of Andrija's Space Kids, for the purpose of driving a unified shaft of energy—a slide of light—into a higher dimension. A lovely young woman named Susan told us she felt unworthy to be part of the group. She had no idea, she said, what her "mission" was to be.

At that point, to Susan's considerable surprise, Tauri appeared. Tauri suggested that we go into the woods. We did, with Susan at my left and Dick to my right.

Tauri had some words of comfort. "If you ride the merry-go-round and you reach for the brass ring and you catch it, that's fine. If you ride the merry-go-round and you reach for the brass ring and you miss it, don't let your music stop, because, remember, merry-go-rounds come round again and you have another chance at the ring."

Then Tauri asked Susan to look up at the one opening in an otherwise cloudy sky. She went on, "Look straight up and tell me how many stars do you see in that one clearing?"

"I see four," Susan said.

"I am going to show you how my energy can move clouds," Tauri declared, and then she snapped my fingers above Susan's eyes. "How many stars do you see now?"

"Six!"

"How many now?" Tauri asked, snapping my fingers twice this time.

"Eight!"

"Ah. So you saw a wondrous thing, did you? Now, is it enough that I feel you have every right to be here? I tell you for your own head, do not worry about being dropped from the group, and do not worry about staying and being incapable of contributing. You have not had the experiences of my channel but you are right to be here with your sensitivities. Yes, I say it is a good thing you be here, child with the beautiful eyes. Now, look at the sky"—two snaps of the fingers— "and what do you see?"

"Ohh," Susan sighed. "Back to only four stars. How . . . how do you do that?"

(This was Susan's first encounter with Tauri, and not her last. She was with me when a magnificent spaceship—one of the "gattae"—was brought in at above-tree-level in Ossining, N.Y. As she put it, "It knocked my socks off!" (It also knocked out all electricity on Puharich's compound!) Susan settled down sufficiently to discover her own "mission," and has since married and gone to live in London, England. She was a major contributor to the success of that Mind Link at which I was the channel.)

On three other occasions Tauri moved clouds, in each case to illustrate a point in as dramatic a fashion as possible. One of those for whom the act was performed was a skeptical Harvard medical resident who demanded absolute proof of the reality of extraterrestrials. He was, suffice it to say, persuaded. It's not easy to remain a skeptic when clouds are moved on a stormy, thundering night to reveal a patch of stars in a portion of the sky selected by the viewer!

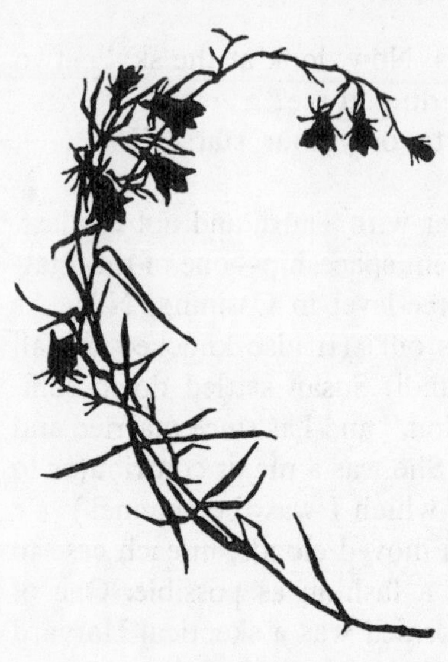

10

TAURI CONTINUED to make her presence known. She would stop in for brief chats on regular occasions. Once she told us that Maya (Ann) was from Oshan and Jilliano (Jill) from Tchauvi.

Dick asked the obvious question. "They're my daughters. How come they don't go back to Ogatta with us?"

"They're not your daughters out here. Only down there."

One evening, Dick and I finished eating and walked into the living room. "Irving," our English marble falcon, sat between the two ottomans on the floor. We had no idea how he got there—until the next afternoon, when Tauri playfully informed us that she had moved (teleported) it herself. She said she liked the "bird" because it reminded her of somebody, though she wouldn't say whom.

We were eating at a local restaurant later that month when I started hearing music. I asked Dick if he heard it, but he didn't. Then I said, "You're supposed to tell me how far the moon is from the Earth and how far Vesta is from the Earth. I don't know why, but that's the message I get."

Dick knew the answer to the former but not the latter. Both of us knew further messages were on the way, so we finished our meal and returned home. At eleven o'clock Tauri spoke, saying, "I think she did very well with that telepathic message tonight. That was the first time she got it right."

"How far is Vesta from here?" Dick wanted to know.

"I told her that you're supposed to know. You can find it out."

"Okay. Whose music was playing?"

"That was our music but I had a reason for putting that into a message. Our channel must learn to know her music. Our music. And now, I'm going to tell you something very strange but it's a fact. Do you know why we are on Vesta for the coming of the gattae?"

"Because it's a staging area, you said."

"We're on Vesta because Ogatta decided it was a better place for this way station than your moon. And do you know that a lot of things were built up there by the Ogatta people? There are gorgeous, beautiful structures up there on the moon. Do you know that a lot of people in the NASA know that? Do you know that they had to be very careful in plotting where your spacecraft landed so as not to disturb it? And do you know that some of your astronauts know it? Do you know that under microscopy they have pictures of them?

"But nobody on Earth knows specifically that they were built by the beings on Ogatta, for the coming of the gattae. Later on, Ogatta decided he'd use Vesta. I am telling it to you tonight and you can tell the "Good Doctor" [Andrija] if you wish. This is my present to you tonight."

"Thank you, Tauri."

"When she starts to talk and to write, maybe it would be a good thing to contact somebody who knows about the structures on the moon. Then it would be much more digestable to the people on your planet Earth. Don't you think so?"

"I think it would. Do you mean to have these scientists here when Greta speaks about it?"

"No! I am saying that maybe you should contact some of the people at the NASA and maybe you should talk to one or two of your astronauts, because they know. Then, when she speaks about the coming of the gattae, these people will know although they never, ever said anything. They all had to take a secret oath. But they know and it didn't matter—*until now.* Do you understand?"

"Yes. It's very important."

"Bridges and all kinds of things they built there, because I know about that. I was not there but I was on Ogatta and I know what they built there."

"What else did they build there?"

"All kinds of landing places and domes and things. They are shiny and silvery and beautiful. We don't have anything that fancy on Vesta, you know, because we didn't need it on Vesta."

"Why did you need it on the moon and not Vesta?"

"I don't know why they did that up there and I don't know why they decided not to use them, but there are lots of things about that moon that nobody knows about."

"Can you tell me some of the other things?"

"I tell you that they know and there are all kinds of records at the N-A-S-A, NASA! . . .

"Your people at the NASA and a few of your astronauts should be pushed to give her validity when she starts to talk and to write. Let me tell you that it is a fact that they are completely convinced that the structures were not made by humans! Do you understand the significance of what I say to you? They know it was done by extraterrestrial beings, made by what they call 'humanoids,' and that is very important for you to think about."

On the occasion of their first meeting in January, Tauri had promised Ann that she would be under Maya's protection during her coming travel abroad. Ann appreciated the sentiment, but since she had no traveling plans in the foreseeable future, she couldn't help being skeptical.

Soon afterward, however, she decided that travel seemed a temptation she couldn't resist. She was a high-school senior at the time and had just received her early admission to Dartmouth. Having enough credits to graduate a semester early, she thought she would take this once-in-a-lifetime opportunity to spend some time abroad before entering college in the fall. She opted to omit her last semester and planned a six-month trip out of the country.

In April she was in Israel. We received the following letter from her.

Dear Mom and Dad:

Danny [a friend she met on the trip] and I were returning to Kiryat Ata from Mount Carmel at twelve forty-five. We were in an Israeli invention known as the "sherut," which is like a taxicab which follows the bus routes, picks up passengers at the stops, and charges per seat. It costs less than private cabs, is a great deal roomier (seating only seven), and goes faster.

Our sherut was full and was swinging down the winding road two kilometers from the central part of Haifa, when a car approached us, coming from around a curve. From that moment it seemed as though the accident took place in slow motion for me. My instinct was to throw my arm in front of Danny's body to brace him from lunging forward. Running through my mind was the thought that we were in the most suicidal seats, since Dan was directly behind the driver and I was next to him in the middle seat. A bar runs across the back of the sherut behind the driver's seat for middle-seat passengers to hold onto. My right hand went to the bar and my left went up to protect Danny. We were going about thirty miles per hour; I let out a scream and turned my head to Danny just before the car was about to hit us.

The next thing I knew, I was looking down at the accident. Mom, Dad, I know that sounds crazy, but it's true. It was as though I had been lifted somehow out of my body and allowed to watch the collision. Immediately after the sherut and car crashed, the next thing I remembered was being on the other side of the street, walking with Danny in the opposite direction of the wreck. I had no recollection of how we got there, nor did I feel injured, despite the obvious minor lacerations I could see. Danny turned to me and in his broken English (he's a Russian immigrant, you know) asked me if I had somehow "seen the accident from above or the sky." His question shocked me speechless! The same thing had happened to him!

I knew I was being protected in Israel, because of what Tauri had said when I first met her, but the shock of the situation was that Danny had experienced the same thing and had questioned me without it fazing him in the least!

Don't worry about me. I was more than fortunate—we both were—to walk away with just minor lacerations, considering the aftermath of the accident. The head-on collision shattered the front windshield and caused the instant deaths of the driver, the front-seat passenger, and the left back-seat passenger. The other three were injured and hospitalized.

We went to the hospital for a routine check and to have our lacerations treated, and after answering police questions, we were released, being told it was a "miracle you survived the crash the way you did." I was shook up but I don't know what did it more . . . the fact that three were killed? . . . the fact that Danny and I both experienced what we did? . . . the fact that I had been told in January that Tauri (or was it Maya?) would watch me during my traveling? . . . All I know is that I was protected somehow and I am here to tell you that all is fine.

What was even more astonishing was that, at the exact time the accident was occurring, Tauri was telling us that Ann was "safe and sound thanks to Maya's intervention at the time of a car accident." Tauri assured us there was nothing to worry about, but that we should be expecting a call from an anxious Ann.

Sure enough, the call came. Needless to say, Ann was flabbergasted that we already knew the reason for her call! Tauri had come through—not for the last time.

Tauri also had something for our son Alan. She and Alan were talking when Alan jokingly said, "When you come, we'll arrange a ticker-tape parade for you."

"What is a ticker-tape parade?" she asked.

Dick explained, "That's where they throw little pieces of paper at you!"

"I don't want anybody to throw little pieces of paper at me! I can throw feathers at you."

With those words my hands waved through the air and when I brought them down, there was a feather in them. "That one for Alan," Tauri said. Then another one materialized, this one intended for Dick. Tauri told them it was from the back of a dove-like Ogattan bird called the kitzber.

Dick and Alan were, needless to say, astonished.

Some weeks later, while Dick was away on business, Alan came over with a cup and a poem, silly but loving, intended for Tauri. Tauri was surprised and pleased. She said she had never gotten a present from any Earthperson before. Because she had "few possessions," she wanted to take the cup back with her to Vesta to show Maya, Lexitron, and maybe Hshames. She would use the cup, she told us, to store moisture or loops.

No sooner had she said that than the cup dematerialized. It had been wrapped in paper, which remained undisturbed. But the cup was gone and the wrapping crumbled at the touch. The three of us stared at each other in amazement.

The following day, however, she returned it, saying she could not keep it or bring it to Ogatta to show him. But she said she would tell him about it.

As Alan was leaving that evening, Tauri gave us a gift: a showering of firna, the lovely lilac-like scent we always associated with her, flowing from a wave of her (my) fingers.

11

"NO ONE EVER HAD a birthday like mine," Dick remarked. He wasn't talking about the party the children and I threw for him, though that was nice. What he was talking about were the guests we had: five friends from the Ogatta group, Tauri, Bilakka, Zeoker, Cjork, and Omee. All stopped in to visit and express their birthday best wishes.

The next day Dick was out working in his garden, lamenting his tardiness that year in buying seeds and plants. Because he was late, he wasn't able to purchase seeds for the yellow acid-free tomato plants he enjoys. It wasn't a big thing, but it was a small pleasure and he was regretting that he would have to pass it by till next year.

When he looked up, there was Zeoker in the channel, intently studying his plants. Zeoker, a botanist from Archa, showed Dick by example what he could do to improve his pruning. (Archans do not speak.) Then he stepped over to examine the tomatoes. Dick told him that the tomatoes were not acid free. Zeoker, through pantomime, indicated that Dick could indeed eat these tomatoes.

Tauri came in to say, "My dear Dick, he wants to give you a present on your day of being. It might be fun for you to get those [litmus] papers to test yourself." And he did. Dick ate the tomatoes without trouble the rest of the summer.

That afternoon another Ogattan, Omee, who works with birds, asked Dick if he would like to see a stilvah, which has the body of a mynah bird but the long legs of a flamingo. Dick nodded excitedly.

Omee was as good as her word. Instantly a stilvah appeared, hanging from the garden enclosure. In a pine tree close by, a second one was staring at him. They were visible for a few moments. Omee said, "Happy birthday, Dick," and they vanished.

What makes Omee's visits even more incredible is that she speaks in a high soprano range. Due to a horseback-riding accident almost forty years ago, my own voice turned very husky. I cannot sing or scream. And yet, when I am channeling and Omee is speaking, she is able to manipulate my damaged vocal cords in such a way that I can reach those extremely high-pitched notes.

No sooner had the stilvahs gone than an Oshanian, Cjork, sprinkled Dick with firna and a kind of warm vibration that stayed with him all day. Dick's arm, which had been aching from a fall, was suddenly healed. Cjork smiled one last time and was gone.

One of the most delightful evenings we ever spent with our Ogattan friends occurred later that month. It all came about because we thought it would be fun to celebrate three birthdays —Dick, Jonathan, and Jill all were born in July—with a night out on the town in the Big Apple.

The four of us started out with dinner at Trader Vic's, an elegant Polynesian restaurant in the Plaza Hotel in Manhattan. We made an early reservation to eat, at five forty-five, so that we could enjoy a leisurely meal before taking in the Yul Brynner revival of *The King and I,* for which Dick had obtained first-row-center orchestra seats.

At dinner I sat in a big butterfly-shaped chair with its back to the wall. Jill sat to my right, Jonathan to my left, and Dick directly opposite me. It was a warm family occasion—and very soon we were to be joined by members of our extended cosmic family.

Midway through the meal Tauri came in to wish Jill and Jonathan happy birthdays. A couple of tables away a baby was crying. Tauri quickly quieted him with a flutter of her fingers in his direction, then spoke to Jill and Jonathan separately. Shortly thereafter Zeoker joined the party. Though he never spoke, he communicated by bows, smiles, and nods, and he was always—amazingly—understood. Zeoker had a special gift for Jill.

Using my body, of course, he leaned forward and extended his hands. In the middle of a public restaurant, a very large green leaf suddenly materialized in the right hand. He offered it to Jill, who clutched it to her as if fearing it would dematerialize any second. She and Jonathan both asked if the leaf came from Archa and Zeoker nodded, sweeping his hands in a gesture of giving.

After that memorable meal the four of us—I was Greta again, briefly—set off for the Uris Theater. We were crossing Broadway at Fifty-first Street when Dick, Jill, and Jonathan realized someone else had joined them, someone they didn't recognize. They knew only that the visitor was male and from Archa; that was clear from the distinctly Archan manner (a waddle) in which the stranger was moving.

The visitor stared hard at Jill, who then asked him if he knew what kind of leaf she had. In response he took the leaf from her hand, held it between his hands as if it were a cob of corn, and nibbled straight across it, his teeth rat-a-tatting like a beaver's! That accomplished, he smiled amiably and gave the remains back, as if to indicate that he didn't recognize them.

I can imagine what passersby must have thought. Here was a demented soul with a strangely quizzical, birdlike expression, eating a gigantic leaf, hunched over and oblivious to such things as cars and traffic lights. Jonathan and Dick were on either side of me, making sure I went where they, safety, and common sense dictated.

We entered the Uris Theater and stepped onto the escalator, where the visitor became entranced with the red hair of a woman on the moving step just above him. He reached out and calmly began to stroke it—to the astonishment, you can imagine, of all. The woman turned around to gape at my scrunched, birdlike face with huge bright eyes. They never told me as much but I strongly suspect one of my birthday darlings hastened to explain that I was harmless. Demented but harmless.

Once in the theater proper, the visitor took his (my) seat and settled back to watch the orchestra assemble. My three companions were quite amused at this turn of events—until Jonathan noticed a female friend from college approaching us. Fortunately he saw her before she got to our little group, and he caught her in time to walk her up the aisle, all the while gaily chattering and doing all in his power to keep her from insisting on seeing the rest of his family.

As this was going on, Dick tried to find out who our new friend was. When he motioned for something to write with, Dick gave him a pen. Then he wrote on the program, with his left hand, "They like him very much." "Him" was Richard Rodgers.

At that point, just before the orchestra began the overture, Jonathan returned and read the odd-looking characters that comprised the peculiar message. He asked if he could have the paper because Jill had been given a leaf. The visitor smiled but shook his head no, then folded the paper into a perfect square and placed it between my right thumb and forefinger.

At the conclusion of the overture everyone applauded. Our visitor looked around and, deciding to join the action, raised his arms straight up over his head (directly in front of the orchestra leader, who was bowing) and clapped in much the way a seal would flip its flippers!

When the music was over, I was back—with, as usual, no sense that I'd been gone. "What happened to the overture?" I exclaimed. "Hey, why no overture?" Jill and Jonathan were laughing uproariously. I couldn't see what was so funny about my questions.

I looked down at my hand and noticed the wadded square of paper. I started to say something when it vanished. One moment it was there; the next it wasn't.

Before the second act Tauri whispered that the visitor was named Dryzek. She said he had had a very pleasant time with us. He certainly had given our family a memorable evening.

Another incident involving the Ogattans' love of music took place that year when musician-composer Steven Halpern visited us. Ordinarily, the Ogattans do not interact with visitors to our home, so the episode was especially interesting. After it happened, we asked Dr. Halpern to prepare a brief account:

> I was introduced to Greta and her intergalactic friends. I was invited to receive a "music lesson" and directed to sit at the piano. With the entity Bilakka I discussed theories of tonality and structure, agreeing on the universality of the five-note pentatonic scale, a scale form which allows each tone to be harmoniously consonant with any other. It also leaves room for a "sixth tone" to be perceived in the mind of the listener.
>
> While seated at the piano I was encouraged to demonstrate, but when I attempted to depress the keys, nothing happened! It was as if the ivories were glued in place! Bilakka and Tauri expanded the lesson and broadened the learning experience. (We were not permitted to tape.) I was then beckoned back to the piano. What a transformed instrument!
>
> My fingers rippled effortlessly over the keys and I was aware of a powerful and exhilarating connection with the piano emanating from my solar plexus and heart chakra. The music that resulted was uplifting and exquisitely beautiful. I was told to work with this sense of connection and to practice composing "for the sixth tone" . . . to be heard with the sixth sense. This I did.
>
> I evolved a number of themes and techniques for fingering and pedaling that felt increasingly like "home." Ten months later, while recording an album entitled *Prelude,* I became aware of a presence that felt very much like what I had experienced at Greta's that night. I wordlessly instructed the engineer to switch modes to "record mode." The studio filled with light as I began to play the piano. Complete compositions flowed effortlessly through my fingers. In one nonstop sequence the entire first side of *Eastern Peace* was received and recorded. The recording occupies a special place in my

heart for its beauty and articulation of the "sixth note," but especially for its manifestation as a jewel of interspecies communication.

(Shortly thereafter an Oshanian named Czork was to comment, "When I think of music, I don't think of music the way you do. There is a matter of harmonics that is foreign to your vocabulary. We of the Ogatta group can see the music as well as hear the music. Art and music blend together into one band. Colors blend in also . . . with music and art. They vibrate. They tingle. If you had a piece of silver tinsel that hung in midair and it shimmered . . . and it began to sing . . . and a beautiful aroma enveloped it . . . would that be an odor, a color, or a sound?")

Steve's music brings the listener quietly into a state of inner calm and balance. A neurosurgeon, Dr. C. Norman Shealy, of the Shealy Pain and Health Rehabilitation Institute, Springfield, Missouri, describes it as "the first music of its kind . . . perfect for the balancing of mind and body." Halpern's music is used in medical, rehabilitation, healing, and research centers all over the United States. It was very exciting to be the channel when two of the Ogatta group exercised an influence on Steve's tapping into a very special place, from which a different kind of music sprang. (I myself cannot play piano or any other instrument.) Almost a decade later, Steve came to our first S.T.A.R. House conference and played this music for our attendees.

12

BEFORE I RELATE what follows, I want to emphasize that my experiences with extraterrestrial intelligences (E.T.I.) have been almost entirely pleasant. My association has been mostly with Ogattan beings who wish us well, who are working to insure that the Earth and its inhabitants have a future. And 100 percent of the time with them has been extraordinary and wonderful. On one occasion in 1977, however, we encountered an entity who did not share the Ogatta group's desire to help us.

I had known of such mentalities before this because Tauri had told us about them. She had said the universe is populated by all manner of entities of varying outlooks and levels of development. Some of them do not want the effort to be put in to save the Earth—not because they are evil but because they have other priorities. That, of course, is understandable. All of us know that we live in a world in which there is much suffering and it is simply impossible to help everyone in need. We may therefore choose to help needy persons who are closer to home rather than, say, people in a remote Third World country.

The analogy may not be exact, since most of us would not

actively oppose efforts to help people in a distant land. But the effort that is going into the coming of the gattae is an enormous one, involving the resources of twenty-four civilizations and an immense concentration of "entity power," time, and energy. It is the view of some extraterrestrial civilizations that it is foolish to engage in this effort when there are so many other urgent things that must be done closer to home.

There are times when cosmic contacts have seemed more like way-out science fiction than our experienced reality. The following story really happened, although to this day whenever we talk about it, it seems beyond belief. This encounter was not with someone from the Ogatta group but with an entity at the same level of evolution as our friendly inhabitants of the Ogatta jorpah. As they explained, there are projects closer to their home planets that need doing and, in the opinion of this group, deserve a higher priority than helping little planet Earth. To this end they set about trying to persuade the Ogatta group to drop its involvement here and put its efforts further out into the cosmos. Their efforts at persuasion took the strange form of dissuasion of the Ogattan channels.

One evening around eleven o'clock a strange entity came calling. I was in bed when he entered the channel and walked into Alan's bedroom in another part of the house to awaken him and make him an offer.

Thornis was an entity from a place called Lathea. He told Alan that if he could discourage his mother from any participation in the Ogattan effort, then, and only then, would *he* be "given the powers of materialization and dematerialization." These powers he could use for any purpose, in or out of business. Thornis suggested to a now very wide-awake twenty-four-year-old that he tell his mother he would take over for her, relieving her of the many pressures associated with the task she had taken on. He, Alan, could deliver the messages to the masses and use his powers to dazzle the audiences and emphasize his points, but obviously not as a channel of the Ogatta group.

"Imagine!" Thornis said. "Now you see something, now you don't!" He went on to say that this gift would always be available to summon up at will. While the offer made his heart race, Alan suspected that it was a scam. He took it as proof of my future effectiveness in "trumpeting the voice and scribing the pen." Dick said it was a divide-and-conquer strategy. And Tauri, when she came in not long afterward, remarked that they had "chosen the channel very carefully." She was bright-eyed with Alan's decision to turn down the offer.

Truth is to tell, I felt that my son would have been equally effective, if not more so. He was articulate, young, and handsome. Alan and his father would not listen.

"The Latheans simply prefer that those who survive be done with it," Tauri said, alluding to the coming tribulations and Earth changes which will wipe out much of our planet's population. "They are saying, 'Best they don't survive.' They disagree with our using channels through whom we give a message of hope and of new technologies.

"We of the Ogatta group and many other civilizations say those who have survived have earned the right to a peaceful survival *with all the help they can get*—thus the 'coming of the gattae.'

"It is much like one of the underdeveloped countries on your planet. The U.S.A. could well say, 'They're far away—let them take care of themselves.' But they don't. They [the United States] send food and money, technology and people, because they feel that they are people who deserve the right to learn and live, even under primitive conditions.

"So, if your condition changes, there are those who think you have earned that right to survival. And others simply feel that 'they brought themselves to it; so be it.' It's that simple."

In a channeling a month later, Tauri returned to the subject of the Latheans. "I do want to clear up what might be a misconception for you. Lathea is on the same dimension as the Ogatta group. I would not want you to think of them as 'the opposition.' They really are not. Their opinion is different from ours on the way planet Earth must come to its conclusion and to its survival pattern. It is the feeling of twenty-plus civilizations of whom we are aware, that help should be sent through the gattae to those survivors. We are very much a part of that program.

"The Latheans, among many others, feel that help should not necessarily be given. That does not mean that they are the opposition—because, you see, they would do nothing to hurt the survivors. There is a difference, subtle though it may be. Understand that!

"Understand what opposition is and what it is not. Very seldom will you really have interference from those terribly concerned with the destruction of your planet. Most often the interference comes from those who simply don't care to see us help it. That's not opposition. That's simply another opinion of what is going to be.

"And in speaking of what's going to be, the time is not that far off that the technology of materialization and dematerialization will be yours on planet Earth."

Alan never had regrets on turning down the offer from Lathea. He was and is a firm supporter of our roles in the scheme of things as they are. He is a major S.T.A.R. supporter. He has turned into a fine healer in his own right, "power-packing" for his mother and with his father in healing work. No divide and conquer there! And if thoughts of "Now you see it, now you don't!" dance in his head, he never mentions it.

13

THE FIRST TIME I ever bent metal paranormally, Dick and I were with Andrija and several other friends and associates at a farm near Devotion, North Carolina, in September of 1977. We were listening to Andrija speak on the work in which we were all engaged. I happened absentmindedly to be holding a spoon in my hands—I was drinking coffee—and at some point I realized that the spoon was starting to bend.

Andrija, who through his work with Uri Geller was an old hand at this sort of thing, calmly suggested that I put the spoon down because, now that it had been energized, it would continue to bend on its own, without my having to hold it.

We placed it on some books behind us and Andrija resumed his talk. About ten minutes later we looked back and it was gone! It had dematerialized.

As we were discussing this unexpected development, Tauri came in and said in a good-humored voice, "I don't know why you concern yourselves with its disappearing. Look to your left. Look to your right. Ha ha!"

Moments later we found the spoon in a different place from

where we had put it. Andrija, who picked it up and examined it, noted that the spoon was more bent than it had been and was now not just bending but twisting. What a combination: deformation and materialization!

A few days later, back in Westport, without touching it, a fork bent under my hand as Tauri was occupying the channel and Dick and Alan were looking on. Tauri used the bending as a dramatic example of what can be accomplished through the focussing of energy—an essential condition for the success of our mission for the Ogattans.

There were several other metal-bending incidents soon afterward, but these were all warm-ups for what was to happen in the place that Tauri insisted on calling the "land of ices," known to us Earthlings as Iceland. I had been invited to attend the Frontiers of Physics Conference, where scientists from the United States and European countries were to present papers describing research into the effect of mind on matter. Tauri had told us that this was going to be a major opportunity for all of us. Referring to the conference, she said, "I want her on her feet. I want her to start to get the word out . . . when you have all of your scientists together." ("Wrong!" I thought to myself. "I'll strictly be an observer and see what I can learn.")

On the way to the airport that November, Tauri came in to talk with Dick about his and my role at the Reykjavik, Iceland, meeting: "Do not feel that your [Dick's] role is confined to watchdog. It is not so or you would not be going to Iceland! . . . She has given some wondrous demonstrations for you people. That's so there need never be doubt in your minds—ever."

Unfortunately, getting there was no easy operation. Or maybe "unfortunately" is not the appropriate adverb, because cancelled flights, stalled traffic, derailed trains, missed arrivals and departures, and similar catastrophes have a way of triggering psychic activity for me. But Dick and I weren't the only ones with problems. Andrija, who was scheduled to host the conference, missed flights in two European countries and didn't arrive at Reykjavik's Loftleider Hotel until two days later than planned.

So we were there well ahead of him. Because we, nonscientists, had come at Andrija's personal invitation and knew practically nobody there, we were made to feel out of place, particularly by uptight American and British scientists who made little secret of their resentment at our presence at their "closed" conference. This was ironic, since a principal reason for the conference was supposed to be the narrowing of the gap between scientists and the rest of the world.

I have come to suspect that the Ogattans wanted things to be that way, maybe even made them that way, feeling this was a perfect spot to display the focussing of energies. All I know for certain is that all of a sudden metal was bending everywhere around me: at the table where we were eating, at coffee breaks, in hotel rooms and corridors. There was no ignoring it and soon even the most conservative and hostile scientists were paying attention. When at last he arrived, Andrija was told that "the polarization ended when metal started to bend."

The conference was a source of fascination to the Icelandic press, which did everything it could to infiltrate the meeting. Some of the participants were prominent Icelanders who did not want their presence publicly known. Others were American and European scientists who, ever fearful of their reputations, were keeping their investigations a secret to all but a handful of trusted colleagues.

One example of the extreme paranoia that afflicts scientists involved in parapsychological investigations took place the second morning of the conference. Physicist Russell Targ, who had received considerable flack for his work at the Stanford Research Institute with Uri Geller, informed me that he had never actually *seen* metal bend. Would I do it for him? When I agreed, he and a colleague picked three identical spoons which nested perfectly inside the other. Targ offered me one of the spoons but I refused to touch it. I asked Targ's companion, physicist Elizabeth Rausher, to hold the spoon.

Then inside my head I thought, "Shrink!" I was not taking myself entirely seriously, but one of the spoons did become smaller. Two other persons, both scientists, were looking on and witnessed the shrinking.

I turned to Targ and said, "Now can you say that you saw metal bend?"

Even though he had selected the spoons himself, he refused to commit himself. "Well," he replied, "this is a hallway, not a laboratory. It was not done under proper scientific conditions."

I wasn't going to let him off that easily. "Did you see metal bend?" I demanded.

"No, I only saw it shrink," he said. Really!

He never recorded this event in any of his scientific papers. He refused to commit his observations to paper, on or off the record, for me. (This sort of infuriating timidity does the progress of human knowledge no good whatever. Targ is typical of those scientists who ask, "Can it be replicated?" whenever they hear of a paranormal feat. Maybe yesterday metal bent in a respectable lab, adhering to "scientific conditions" and measured by strain gauges, but if it doesn't bend on command today, then yesterday's achievement is called into question. Science demands empirical data and those data are compiled through repetitive testing. Psi, the international word and symbol, cannot always be delivered on command; it is, by definition, paranormal, beyond today's rules of what is considered normal. If scientists are unwilling to make allowances for its vagaries, they will never find it, even though it is all around us.) Other renowned scientists and physicists, however, were willing to commit to paper what they had witnessed, and for this I was grateful.

Weeks later, Tauri would input, "We have said to you that *science* is *cosmic revelation.* One of the problems with human beings is that they use science as an attempt to define. Once you define something, you lose more than you gain because to define something scientifically means there is a finality. But there is nothing final."

Another event that occurred there at the conference made us ill in quite a literal sense. It happened after the day's scientific presentations, when we went to our rooms. It had been a fascinating, exciting day and we were feeling magnificently happy. We commenced to play our usual game of backgammon before we went to bed. Suddenly I started to cry and shake all over. Dick doubled up, nauseated and dizzy. The attack, horrible and utterly unanticipated, lasted for forty-five minutes. We could hardly believe it. Things like this didn't happen to us. Seasoned travelers, we were unused to getting sick in strange countries. And the illness was a peculiar one, unlike any we had ever experienced anywhere.

The next morning the illness had passed. At the conference Dr. Puharich asked everyone whether anything unusual had happened during a certain forty-five-minute period the evening before—the same period in which we had gotten sick. As it turned out, only two persons had been unaffected, a couple who had gone elsewhere for the night. The rest reported weakness, nausea, deep depression, and crying jags.

Dr. Puharich then explained. From Riga, Latvia, the Russians had been beaming extra-low frequency (ELF) radiation at that time. Was the conference the target? The disabling response that hit us at Reykjavik is precisely the response these ELF frequencies are meant to cause. At the time we were hit, the Soviets were in the early experimental stages. Apparently our conference was attracting attention of the most unwelcome kind. Or was it just an accident? A coincidence? As someone once said, "Coincidences are the visible traces of untraceable principles."

As the conference progressed it became necessary to accommodate Iceland's curious reporters. Several scientists and researchers agreed to talk with reporters, and it was decided that the press would gather in Andrija's hotel suite. As fate would have it, practically everybody was off on a sightseeing trip that day and there were transportation problems. So when the reporters showed up, there was only Andrija, anxiously pacing up and down the floor with Christopher Bird, author of *The Secret Life of Plants* and *The Divining Hand,* and waiting for the scientists to return.

At that moment I was wandering down the hallway trying to get back to my room. Since all the doors looked the same, I was confused, and I ended up opening a door which I thought was mine but which turned out to be Andrija's. I wandered into the suite and Andrija, a look of enormous relief on his face, waved me over. He introduced me to the reporters, saying I had bent metal for almost everybody at the conference.

Of course the reporters immediately asked me to bend metal for them, but I refused to do so, not wishing to be the center of attention. Assuming that everybody would be back at any moment, I killed time by lightheartedly describing my experiences in Iceland.

When nobody showed and the clock ran on, the reporters got more and more impatient. Finally, exasperated, they informed us that Iceland's television had only three fifteen-minute news segments: at 9:00 A.M., noon, and 8:00 P.M. This last newscast, in prime time, was the most popular, and the television journalists had hoped to highlight the story in this time slot—and time was running out.

So I relented. The following story (inelegantly translated) appeared as the lead on Iceland's 8:00 P.M. TV news.

> Can flowers be spoken to? Can diseases be healed and can spoons bend all by the power of the mind alone? Has the human mind access to an inexplicable power which can remove ills from the living body and find hidden objects in the bowels of the Earth?
>
> At a press conference held at Hotel Loftleider at two o'clock today, an American lady named Greta Woodrew showed to reporters cases of her abilities in this field by bending two teaspoons in their presence. The reporters who came to the press conference at the hotel today were rather incredulous when they were shown two teaspoons, one of which had been bent by Mrs. Woodrew by holding it in her hand and rubbing it gently before the eyes of forty scientists from several countries who have been discussing, in a number of sessions during the whole week, phenomena that belong to the verge or frontier of physics.
>
> Truly, these events have occurred under the strictest control of the scientists, and a number of such phenomena have now received the recognition of the scientists on both the western and eastern side of the Iron Curtain.
>
> When the reporters asked Greta Woodrew to repeat the experiment, the scientist present, Puharich, who had convened the conference, said that it would depend upon the positive attitude and easy

mood of the persons present whether results could be expected. But the following pictures were taken at the press conference today.

Television viewers saw me take a teaspoon, balance it on my fingertip and rub it gently with another finger, whereupon the spoon slowly bent. I put it down on the table beside another, unbent spoon and the difference between the two was clearly apparent.

At the conference Greta had succeeded in bending a teaspoon which lay on a table just by knocking lightly under the table, and without touching the spoon on the upper side at all. This was judged to be very important by the scientists.

When coffee was served at the press conference today, Greta said that the atmosphere was better than she had expected and she placed her hand under the table beneath one of the saucers where a teaspoon lay on its edge. The reporters could hardly believe their own eyes when the teaspoon began to bend, while Greta rubbed and knocked gently on the lower surface of the table. In this picture we can see the difference between the spoons that lay on the table when this happened.

Greta Woodrew says of herself that she cannot scientifically explain the energy which enables her to bend metals, but she feels that something unknown stands behind her efforts. At the press conference today we ultimately met some highly reputable scientists from both east and west of the Atlantic who are active in this kind of research . . .

A thin rail of wire [Nitinol, developed at the Naval Surface Weapons Center in Maryland] was shown to reporters which was made of a mixture of titanium and nickel which seems to have a "memory." This property of the metal is used in making antennae for spacecraft. When the rail is given its first form at a certain temperature—say at a very high or low grade on our everyday scale—and wrapped up at room temperature, it can then take back its first form again. (The metal is a member of a new class of materials known as Shape Memory Effect alloys. Uri Geller has "destroyed the memory" in the past. Greta "destroyed" the memory today by simply touching it!) Now we see the rail as it looked today.

Indeed, few things seem impossible when we enter these fields. Thus the mind-benders, if we may say so, bent a support from titanium which is being used in the Concorde. We are told that this was being done under stringent scientific control. And indeed, no observation indicated that for this act any force had been applied except the inexplicable force of the mind which the reporters came to witness at the press conference.

The news story caused a sensation in Iceland. Dick and I were scheduled to leave Reykjavik the next morning, but again transportation difficulties caused a delay. Press and television accounts had suggested (correctly) that the energy that bends metal can also be used to heal, and this brought scores of people suffering from all kinds of afflictions to our hotel, all asking for help.

Again the travel difficulties sparked my psychic abilities. In the next twenty-four hours I did healings both at the hotel and, in response to a request by our host, Icelandic scientist Gudmundur Einarrsson, at the dying ward of a local hospital. It was a whirlwind of activity and the newspapers covered it on their front pages, sometimes misquoting me but at least getting the essentials right. Later an Icelandic friend wrote to say that "this type of happening" had never received so much attention or caused so much excitement before. Healing is a subject with which everyone should be familiar. I will get into its history, the how-to's, and some of my experiences later on.

One incident that occurred at the hospital boggled my mind. I had agreed to the request that the leading psychic artist in Iceland be allowed to accompany us on our healing rounds and quietly sketch the proceedings. We paid no attention to her as we went from room to room, Dick always sitting behind me and Gudmundur, the scientist, at the foot of each bed while I stood next to the patients.

I entered the final room and was struck by the weakness and pallor of the woman propped up on her pillows and trying to smile. She appeared to be in the last throes of her fatal illness. I wanted very much to help her in some way. I always begin my healing sessions with a silent prayer. And then, since color represents a distinct and measurable quantity of energy, I think of a color in the visible spectrum. (It was Dr. Albert Einstein who defined the quantity of energy in the visible spectrum, for which he was awarded a Nobel Prize in Physics in 1920.) I project this discrete packet of energy, this color, to the patient. No one in the world would know about this concept of mine except Dick.

This night, I decided that instead of a high color (blue, indigo, even white) a lower, more engulfing, less energetic color was called for in my imaging. Behind me, I knew Dick would be holding violet for me in mind. My feet firmly planted on the ground, I "threw red." The healing went on and the woman regained some bloom in her cheeks.

When it was over and we left the room, the interpreter with us said the psychic artist (who spoke no English) wanted to know why the healer used red on the patient. "I never knew a healer to use the color red before," she said. "Her husband sent her a violet light and Mr. Einarrsson was meditating with yellow. But red is strange, very strange."

I almost fell over when Gudmundur admitted that he was indeed trying to envision the patient in a haze of gold. Dick nodded assent to the violet. How did that artist accurately call those colors? Her answer was straightforward and simple: "I could see the auras clearly. Red just flowed from her hands, you know. It's amazing to see the patient look stronger after it, no?"

Into the stunned silence she added, "Nine holy figures stood behind the healer. See, look at my drawing."

She handed me a beautiful pastel sketch done with stick figures: red emanating from the healer, violet from the man behind her, yellow from the figure at the foot of the bed. Nine hooded figures with halo-like lights were lined up behind the healer. I cannot vouch for the religious figures but I *can* attest to that artist's abilities as a sensitive.

The Frontiers of Physics Conference had been a resounding success on a number of counts. A subsequent paper by Thorsteinn Gudjonsson noted all this and went on to state:

"The results of the physicists at the conference, important as they were, could only have been brought together by such enthusiastic and harmonical meeting as the Frontiers of Physics assembly was, from the beginning to the end. The factor of prime importance for the whole fortunate development was, beyond question, the presence of Ms. Greta Woodrew from the U.S.A. at the conference. Being a dynamic personality herself, Ms. Greta Woodrew recently discovered her mind-metal-bending ability, and this power happily continued to manifest itself during the conference."

When Dick and I got on the plane bound for home, I was physically exhausted. No sooner did the plane leave the runway than I curled up in my seat and fell fast asleep. Dick decided that he wouldn't interrupt my slumber even for meals. The steward on board had other ideas, however.

Because of the extensive television coverage he recognized me. Approaching our seats, he asked Dick if I weren't the "one on TV."

Dick whispered, "Yes," and put his finger to his lips. "She's really very, very tired."

Ignoring Dick and whipping a spoon out of his pocket, the steward leaned over, shook my shoulder and demanded, "Well, if you can really bend metal, let's see you do this spoon!"

I opened a bleary eye and murmured, "I do not think this is the time. Forgive me." I rolled back over toward the window. Incredibly, the steward again reached over and pushed his finger into my shoulder, repeating his demand, "Do it! Do it!"

Dick was speechless. Again, I opened my eyes and repeated, "No, I think not. Thank you for your interest."

The steward put his hands on his hips and angrily addressed the knot of people who were now listening. "Well, I didn't think she could do it anyway," he declared.

This one negative incident notwithstanding, we returned from Iceland exhausted but exhilarated. A few days later Dick and I celebrated our twenty-fifth wedding anniversary. Just before we went out to dinner, a whole procession of Ogattans came through to give us their best (Zeoker did more than that; he materialized a leaf for us). The Ogattans, we learned, were as pleased as we about the developments in Iceland. Practically the first thing Tauri said to Dick was, "I would say she did all right. Bobbled their minds!"

In the decade since our adventure in Iceland, I have stopped deforming metal except on rare occasions. It is an attention-getter, no doubt about it. But the same energy can be used for more important matters, such as healing. And never do I try to "convince" anyone of anything. I simply try to open minds to awesome possibilities. Tauri was right, though: When metal bends, minds are bobbled.

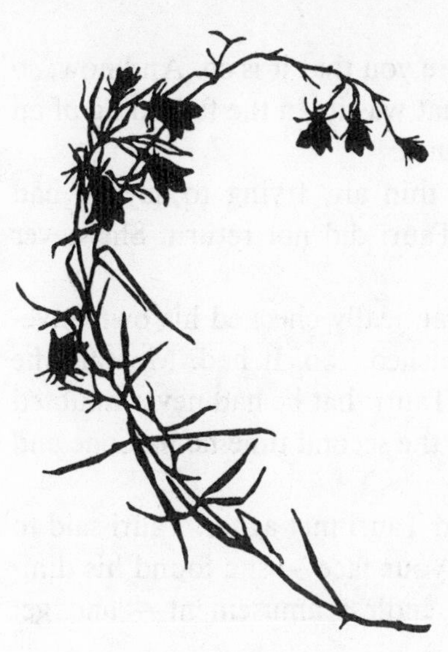

14

ONE EVENING Andrija, Dick, Alan, and I were sitting in our den when Tauri suddenly made an appearance. Dick reminded her of an incident that occurred while we were coming in for a landing in Florida, when Tauri caused a kitzber bird to appear outside the plane, flying effortlessly through the Earthly sky. Tauri chuckled at the memory, remarking on how gracefully the kitzber had flown next to the lumbering of the sea gulls.

She turned to Andrija and Alan and offered to give them each a kitzber feather. They enthusiastically accepted the offer. "Get two envelopes and put one in each of your laps," Tauri insisted. After completion of the task she told them, "Now open the envelopes." Inside each one was a tiny, fluffy, white, incredibly soft feather.

Alan handled his carefully, then placed it back inside his envelope and sealed it. For his part, however, Andrija could not resist observing that the thing looked more like something he called "manna" than it did a feather.

In a tone of mock offense Tauri exclaimed, "Well! If I tell you it is a feather, dear doctor, I assure you that it is so. And now, so much for your 'manna.' " And that was it. In the twinkling of an eye, it was gone. And so was Tauri.

Andrija was apologizing into thin air, trying to say he had made a "terrible mistake," but Tauri did not return. She never mentioned the incident again.

Seeing all this happen, Alan frantically checked his own envelope to see if his feather had vanished, too. It had. Mentally he pleaded to have it back, assuring Tauri that he had never doubted it was a kitzber feather. This was the second time he had one and lost it. He was devastated.

Sometime later, when Alan and Tauri met again, Tauri said to him, "Go, you with the holes in your face"—she found his dimples and cleft chin a source of endless amusement—"and get another envelope."

Alan dashed upstairs and returned with a business envelope in hand.

"Is it empty?" Tauri asked.

"Yes, Tauri."

"Look again."

When he did, he was delighted to find another feather. This one didn't disappear. He kept it for a long time, not showing it even to Dick and me.

At our cosmic twenty-fifth anniversary our four children surprised us with a birdlike bronze statue, sculpted by a local artist and representing a member of the Ogatta group. The statue had sculpted feathers, with wings spread wide. Under the wing-arms were hands. The eyes were large and luminous and on the back the children had the artist put a tiny spaceship. Alan put his precious feather into this little gattae.

In the following weeks our various Ogattan friends dropped by. They all seemed fascinated, but a little bothered, by the statue. Whenever Ogattans wanted to express happiness or approval, they would touch heels together, lift their arms upward, palms up, and put their heads back, in a gesture reminiscent of gymnasts coming off rings, bars, and horse. Dick and the kids had seen the gymnastic-looking gesture many times, but not now. Zeoker in particular was critical of the angle of the neck and the position of the arms, which he indicated were not right.

Over the next three months the statue seemed to be changing. The changes were not instantaneous but they were unmistakable. The neck was arching up and the arms were rising higher into the air. Even our friends were noticing this. Finally I thought I had better show it to the artist who had sculpted it. If anybody could confirm the changes, she could, since before handing it over to our children she had photographed it from every conceivable angle so that she could add it to her portfolio.

So she came over with her pictures. What she found is described in a statement I asked her to prepare:

> I designed an imaginative, humanized, upward-striving eagle, arms and hands reaching toward the sky. I incorporated a small spaceship on its back. The sculpture was modeled directly in wax in August 1977. Using the traditional lost wax method it was cast in bronze in September 1977. At the completion of the sculpture, I took photographs of the piece. The sculpture was then turned over to the four children who had commissioned me to create the piece as a gift from them to their parents. It is prominently displayed in the Woodrew home.
>
> At my recent visit to Greta Woodrew's home, the first thing I noticed was a decided shift in the angle of my eagle bird. This piece of sculpture, being solid bronze, could *not* change on its own at any time, yet comparing it to the pictures I had taken, there is a perceptible change.
>
> Greta, you asked me to write down my impressions after reviewing my piece in your home. I thought you might be interested in hearing about my most unusual observation about my own sculpture. Bronze does *not* change shape, but that bird is definitely in a different position. It is beautiful, but altered.
>
> I loved visiting with you, but I am really not sure that I enjoyed this most perplexing happening for which I have *no* explanation at all.

The figure has continued to alter over the decade, most dramatically at our home, Reisha Way, these last five years. It is a source of conversation and amazed delight to all relatives and visitors who know its history. As of this writing ten years later the head is thrown back, the arms in an Ogattan posture, and it tilts to the right in an appearance of flight.

Since that time I have traveled all over the world, trumpeting the voice and describing the Scenario, and wherever I go, in the audience there is always someone who will jump to his feet and throw me an Ogatta greeting, arms flung upward. It never fails to bring tears to my eyes.

Following our return from Iceland, metal was bending all over the place. For the most part these episodes took place with friends and relatives. They constituted a powerful way of confirming that our lives were changing and that we had some very special friends in high places.

One evening we were dining with friends. Howard was the Director of Communications for IBM—a very literal man. As we waited for the waiter, I picked up a spoon, held it lightly between my thumb and forefinger, and shook it up and down for about thirty seconds. When I put it back down, it had bent (at the bend portion between the handle and the bowl) about half an inch. It caught our friends' attention!

The following day Howard described what happened next:

"Ms. Woodrew then took another spoon, whose configuration I again checked and found to be normal, placed it in a cup, with the handle sticking up at an angle from the cup. Without touching the spoon at all, she ran her hand over it several times, again for perhaps thirty seconds, at which point the spoon handle began to droop down toward the table top. Though she then stopped moving her hand over the spoon, the spoon handle continued to bend and finished with the end of the handle just past the lip of the cup—that is, the handle was just short of being in a "U" configuration.

"Later, at her home, Ms. Woodrew asked one of my sons for his house key. It was a new key I had recently purchased. She put the key in our oldest son's hand, in his half-closed fist, and, as best as I can describe it, also touched the key and commanded it to bend. My son opened his fist and in fact that same key was both bent and twisted. My son was profoundly affected, realizing that he had retained control of the key and had inspected it before putting it in his fist. Neither he nor I could find a rational explanation for this phenomenon . . .

"I should note that I come to this area of activity with rather advanced skepticism. All of these experiences suggest to me that complete skepticism is no longer tenable."

On the very next evening we were invited to dinner by some other dear Connecticut friends of long standing. We intended to broach "the subject"—the Ogattans and their mission—to them. We hadn't said anything about it before. When we started talking with them, we must have sounded pretty disjointed and, I'm sure, unconvincing. They listened politely.

Finally, sensing that the message wasn't getting through, I balanced a sterling silver spoon on top of my finger and watched it bend. Our friends were startled, even more so when I bent—this time without touching it—another sterling silver spoon, this one in a sugar bowl. I didn't touch a third one either: I bent it simply by hitting the table from the bottom, under the spot where the spoon lay. It twisted like a pretzel.

Later our host admitted to us that he would not have been able to believe our story if he had not been "hit between the eyes" with the demonstrations. His wife Betty just murmured, "Oh, my sterling!"

My favorite spoon-bending experience occurred sometime later, when I was lecturing in Minneapolis. An old friend and newspaper publisher asked if I would give a demonstration for a "hard-bitten skeptic" of a newspaperman, Holly Meier. He was described to me as a pure curmudgeon, the hard-boiled managing editor of the Lavine Newspaper Group, a chain of newspapers in the upper Midwest.

He came a complete skeptic. He left and wrote a column published in four Wisconsin newspapers:

I witnessed an exhibition (if, indeed, it can be called that) of spoon- and fork-bending that gives the lie to charges that it is done with trickery.

The woman who proved to me that her mind was stronger than metal was Dr. Greta Woodrew, author of the book *On a Slide of Light,* and she convinced me in a very short time that what she can do is no hoax.

Without retelling the story in too much detail, I can recall how I sat across from Dr. Woodrew with a coffee table between us. She spilled a handful of spoons and forks out on the table in front of me and had me put my hand over them. She then put her hand on mine and told me to think, "Bend."

She did not touch the silverware.

We did it again but this time with spoons and forks I had brought with me from another kitchen.

They were heavy-shanked and almost impossible to bend, even when I tried to do it with both hands.

I put them down on the table and once again Dr. Woodrew put her hand over mine—but didn't touch the silverware.

"Now think, 'Bend,' " Dr. Woodrew said quietly, and I thought, "Bend."

And I once again felt the spoons and forks bend in my hand. And they were twisted all out of shape.

And on the way out of the hotel, we passed a door where somebody had put out a tray of dirty dishes—the leftovers from a breakfast.

Dr. Woodrew reached down and picked up a fork and handed it to me.

It was a perfectly normal-looking fork, with both its tines and handle straight.

I carried the fork down to the lobby and as I said good-bye to Dr. Woodrew, she looked down at the fork in my hand and whispered, "Think, 'Bend!' "

I did, and felt the fork squirm in my hand.

And when I looked at it, the tines were crippled and the handle bent almost in a "U" shape.

And whenever I hear charges that spoon-benders are fakes I take out that fork (as I have right now) and look at it.

And with that fork—and the recollection of how it was bent—I have perfect, positive proof that one woman, Dr. Woodrew, is anything she wants to say she is—except a fake.

Why do spoons bend? Psi forces have gentle characteristics, like gravity. Be easy about it. Keep it light! Remove the shadow of any negative thoughts in the way.

You allow the spoon to bend. You do it by removing the patterns by which it has been set. You're unwinding the field that binds its atoms into those patterns. You're allowing it to bend to the pattern you have envisioned in your mind. Gently you remove the energies that hold it in its present form and allow the atoms the freedom to move into the pattern that you present.

Remove the old patterns and allow the new one to come in. Just as you can talk to plants, you can talk to spoons as well, with love—the greatest positive energy of all. Love the spoon and allow it to bend.

Metal-bending is only one of the new abilities that are becoming available to us—abilities that will be a necessity in the times to come, a criterion of the new life.

I learned these abilities through practice, practice, practice. Nothing worth having comes easily, and certainly those abilities did not come easily. Practice, though, is not the same thing as work. Psi abilities do not respond to effort. They respond to intent, to confidence, to direction, to positive thought, and to the ability to draw energy from the Earth and use it.

You have to learn those abilities. As a child can learn to walk and talk, so too can your psi abilities be brought to light. Potentially you have always had those capabilities. Today they are being stimulated by new frequencies—packets of energy—that are growing in strength, demanding more of you.

Throughout history unique individuals and groups of people have known and used their extrasensory abilities. The stimulation now striking the planet makes them easier to develop. We shall need these sensitivities, this awareness beyond the five senses, in the trying times ahead. This is part of the Scenario of what the "architects of the future" will be able to handle and provide.

Psychic abilities can be turned on overnight, in the face of great need. Or they can be learned and be available when the need is not so great.

Each of you has a story of using psi abilities spontaneously. Necessity called them up; it may have been a small accident that made you miss the plane that crashed; a dream that warned you of a life-threatening situation. You may have known you were needed desperately and gotten there before word could reach you by conventional means.

The Ogatta group talks of using our "positive energy" in the time of transition ahead. The Ogattans say these energies will help us survive the planetary changes that will lead us to a brighter tomorrow. Such positive energy, whether a healing thought or a telepathic communication, will have the final say on all that matters to us. If we wait until tomorrow, we risk the possibility of not learning to handle the energy to be able to summon it up when needed. So practice—now—is essential. How do you do it?

There are many ways. Practice with a plain deck of playing cards, separating them into blacks and reds without looking at the faces. And don't let yourself get discouraged. You're learning a new skill, and if at first you don't succeed . . .

One talent you can cultivate is dowsing. Christopher Bird, author of an encyclopedic work on the subject, *The Divining Hand,* says, "Like expertise on the violin . . . and other virtuosities seemingly inaccessible to the average citizen . . . dowsing can be acquired by the open-minded who have not developed a mindset against the 'obvious impossibility' of so uncanny a searching art."

Chris Bird illustrated it once when we were riding along a dirt road in rural Mexico in August 1978, en route to a conference in Valle de Bravo. We were lighthearted in anticipation of an exciting experience at this second Frontiers of Physics gathering, but the road seemed to go on and on.

"Where the heck are we, and how many kilometers to Valle de Bravo?" an exhausted and exasperated Dick wanted to know.

Chris picked up the road map from the seat, ran his fingers

lightly over the area we were traveling—and told us how far we were from our destination. Despite some good-natured teasing we noted the reading on the odometer and we arrived at the meeting site in exactly the number of kilometers Chris had dowsed.

To dowse is to search with the aid of a hand-held instrument such as a forked stick or a pendular bob on the end of a string—for *anything,* subterranean water flowing in a narrow underground fissure, a pool of oil or a vein of mineral ore, a buried sewer pipe or electrical cable, an airplane downed in a mountain wilderness, a disabled ship helplessly adrift in a gale, a lost wallet or dog, or perhaps a buried treasure.

I lost a gold pendant once and knew it was somewhere in the house. So I drew slips of paper saying, "bedroom, kitchen, hall, living room" and so on, for all the rooms of the house. I used a pendant on a string, decided that a circling motion would mean yes, and up-and-down motion no.

When it answered me "bedroom," I drew a floor plan of the room and dowsed its exact location—under the bed, or, more specifically, under the edge of the rug under the bed.

I recall a story we heard from Icelandic scientist Gudmundur Einarrsson. He had both drilled into the hot geothermal pools that generate energy for the city of Reykjavik and engineered the underground network of pipes that supply the homes and industry of the city.

When the idea of using underground volcanic pools to heat the city was first proposed, the question of how most effectively to locate the drilling sites arose. Finding geothermal pools is very much like drilling for oil, a hit-and-miss proposition. As in oil-well drilling, a ratio of one or two successes in ten attempts is considered average to good. Knowing this and also being a student of the paranormal, Einarrsson decided to use some unorthodox methods to locate the drilling sites. He contacted an American psychic named Frances Farrelly—at the suggestion of our friend Dr. Puharich—and asked her to try to locate the required hot water supply through the ancient method of dowsing.

When Einarrsson invited her to Reykjavik, Farrelly said that she did not need to come to the city; she could locate the water without leaving her home in Florida.

Although somewhat skeptical, Dr. Einarrsson collected maps of the city and surrounding areas and flew with them to Farrelly's home. She spread the maps on her kitchen table and while he drank coffee, she dowsed the maps. Within hours Farrelly had pinpointed the spots for him to drill for the geothermal pools.

Incredible as it sounded to Dick and me, Einarrsson told us that he met with 100-percent success when he drilled in the spots precisely marked by Farrelly.

I met and appeared on a panel with Frances Farrelly later, in Madrid in 1980. She proved to be a delightful lady with a Ph.D., a zest for living, and a sparkling personality. When we asked her to describe her part in finding the geothermal pools in Reykjavik, she smiled and said, "Oh-ho, so you heard about that, did you?"

(Six years were to pass before I dowsed successfully for a much-needed well on our property. Dr. John Shisler, an expert in magnetic radiations, checked out my site and came within inches of the same spot. Today that well produces fifteen gallons of water per minute!)

Another skill available to *all* of us is telepathy. To be able to make use of it, we have to re-learn what we've let atrophy since we became "civilized." The aborigines of Australia have used this skill since prehistory.

Recently the aboriginal elder, Guboo Ted Thomas of the Yuin tribe of Australia, spoke at our S.T.A.R. House. He talked about the continuous many-thousand-year-old relationship his people have with Mother Earth. He talked of how they use their minds to tune into other species, such as trees and animals. Then he said the thing that made me sit up and take notice: They use their minds today to contact one another hundreds of miles away. Imagine—telepathy has been in man's arsenal of awareness for more than forty thousand years. It just suffers from disuse.

In our earliest contacts with the Ogatta Group, we were urged to "learn telepathic skills so that you can communicate with your loved ones when the normal lines of communication are disrupted at the times of the great changes." Tauri explained how:

"Be still! Develop the ability to clear the mind. The easiest thing in the world to do is to send a message out, but it's a bit harder to receive it and understand it.

"Find the right ones to practice with. Someone with whom you are in tune. Tell them to play the game simply—send just a color. A number. A shape. Something simple. Send it out, and when it is received, have it sent back to you. Soon you will find it is quite easy.

"You see, when man plays his tricks on man and nature has her way, communications will break down—communication systems such as you are accustomed to. Wires will fall to the ground, useless. Telephones will not function. The television sets will just be boxes without pictures.

"Do you see what people will need? Mind control for messages to be sent over what you think of as 'distance.' Control the mind's energy! It is necessary, not wondrous, to be able to send and receive a message through the energy controlled by the mind. Eventually you will not need words, just thoughts. Such is our telepathy."

Telepathy should be as casual and useful as the voice communication we mostly depend on now—if you practice.

While Tauri was in the channel one day, Dick asked her, "The abilities to communicate telepathically and handle heightened frequencies of energy—how will my age category of people be able to do that? We use platitudes about practicing and so on, but we're not sold that that's the answer."

Tauri said quickly, "Not all nonsense . . . no! You can practice telepathy and it does get better with this practice. As for overall survival, don't minimize the vibrations—that is a strange word, by the way—that are bombarding this piece of the cosmos."

Vibrations are packets of energy associated with each and every electromagnetic (EM) wave. There are more EM waves on the planet, both man-made and cosmic, than ever before. And they all hit our bodies. How will we handle them?

"The little ones will be more able to handle these heightened vibrations than you can possibly know," said Tauri. "The question is the elders. They must be able to handle them or they will not participate in the changes."

Dick asked, "The elders are in the fifty-year-old category like we are, I take it?"

"Older, younger, both," Tauri answered. "How do you get a sun tan? You do it gradually, not by lying out from 9:00 A.M. to 5 P.M. and getting burned, sizzled, fried, freckled. In order to get the beautiful tan, you do it very slowly, a few moments at a time, until the skin turns a golden shade without harm to the skin. What you must learn to do is get a telepathic sun tan."

Don't make telepathy difficult. Just quickly visualize the person to whom you wish to speak—and speak. It's no more complicated than saying hello or asking someone to go shopping with you.

Just—if you will pardon the expression—reach out and touch someone. Dialing somebody in telepathically is much like dialing a telephone. When you visualize him in his own person, you are in effect dialing his "number," his "pattern," and the call goes through—across the room, across the street, or across the continent.

The Ogatta group tells us that every human being on planet Earth has his own electromagnetic (EM) print. It's easy for the Ogattans to locate us by that EM print. It can be easy for you to locate anyone by his EM print—once you catch on to the trick of it.

It is interesting to note that phrases such as "good vibes" and "bad vibes" are standard slang, expressions we use without reflecting on what they mean. Vibrations, in fact, are all around us. They are electromagnetic in nature and they affect us all.

The big piece of the vibration story comes from other cosmic bodies doing the same mating dance as we circle the center of the Milky Way. By "we" I don't mean just planet Earth, but our entire solar system. (The Earth is less than one-quarter of one percent of the total mass of all the planets, the planets being less than one percent of the solar system, and the sun comprising 99 percent of the solar system.) It is like a giant tug of war with two teams, gravity and electromagnetism, at each end of the cosmic rope. The bigger the cosmic body (star or planet), the stronger the pull of gravity at the end of the rope.

There are two options in this tug of war: to be pulled into the star exerting the force or to exert an equal (but opposite) force and build a relationship of equality at both ends of the mythical rope. The late Buckminister Fuller said that "gravity is concentering." It goes directly to the core, the center of the system—the solar plexus—like a laser beam. And, as in a tug of war, the energy received at the center must be redistributed equally to all parts or the body will be pulled from its position (orbit). This concentering pull "at the end of the rope" is returned as an equal but opposite EM force, keeping the cosmic bodies in equilibrium, holding their positions. The difference is that they are not static with a pool of mud or water between them, but are orbiting around the center of the Milky Way Galaxy.

From time to time, because of differing orbits, the influence of one star gradually gives way to the influence of another star. It's like handing the end of the rope to another person, a bigger person, one who can exert a greater pull on the rope. When this happens, the same two choices exist: to fall in or to handle the greater pull with an equal but opposite force. In the cosmos an equalizing force is exerted. But it changes the energies in the game, the vibrations.

When the Earth takes a stronger pull in its center, it must distribute the energies throughout its body. This can change the geological make-up of the planet by causing mountains to rise and land to shift and possibly disappear. The greater gravitational energy requires a greater EM equalizer. All the vibrations "step up" and the dance around the Milky Way continues.

You can bet that cosmic bodies will handle the changed energies and restore an equilibrium to the tug of war in the sky. The question is, will the species inhabiting the cosmic bodies be able to evolve quickly enough to live and prosper in the higher energy environment?

We are in that vibration-changing period now. Species must be able to learn to handle the increasing energies or become footnotes in history. Science tells us that more than 90 percent of the species that inhabited the Earth went to extinction before the newcomer, man, made his appearance. With the changes in process, confirmed to us by the Ogatta Group, many more of the species that prospered in a lower energy environment will go extinct.

A vibration, an EM wave, a gravity wave—all are measurable packets of energy. When the vibes get higher, we all have to learn to play the game of life in a more charged arena. And since energy is also knowledge, it will be a more exciting, more highly evolved world in which to live. To paraphrase Tauri, "We can't minimize the vibrations that are bombarding this piece of the cosmos."

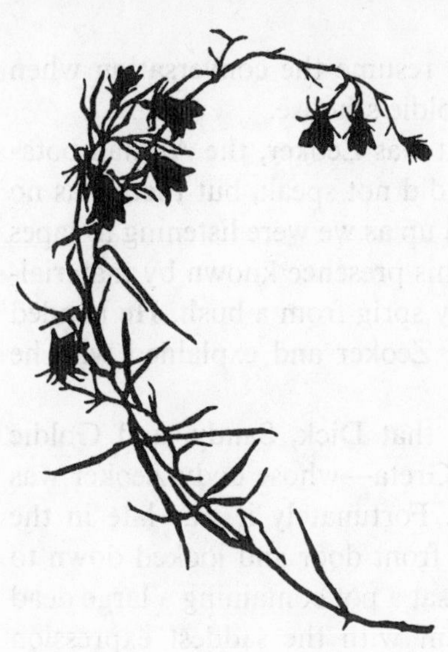

15

IN NOVEMBER 1979, we were in North Miami Beach, Florida, visiting my brother Sandy and his wife Goldie. They knew nothing about our involvement with the Ogattans and we felt it was time to tell them. We staged the "enlightenment" at an elegant restaurant, and I started to discuss the Ogattan mission. In the course of the conversation that followed I bent a heavy stainless steel spoon by tapping the table under it; I also bent two other spoons just by lightly touching them with the pad of my forefinger.

That made an impression on them. By coincidence two friends, store merchants from New York City on a buying trip to the Miami area, were sitting at the table next to us. As the bending was going on, they happened by the table and one exclaimed, in all innocence, "Oh, magic!" Obviously he couldn't imagine that it could be anything else.

Later, Tauri came through and liberally dispensed firna as she laughed and joked with everybody. At one point she asked if her companions would allow her to remove the waiter's mustache!

More seriously, she promised to resume the conversation when we all returned to Sandy and Goldie's house.

But when we got back there, it was Zeoker, the Archan botanist, who appeared. As usual he did not speak, but there was no doubting who he was. He showed up as we were listening to tapes of Tauri's transmission, making his presence known by materializing what appeared to be a shiny sprig from a bush. He handed it to Goldie as Dick introduced Zeoker and explained who he was.

Zeoker made signs indicating that Dick, Sandy, and Goldie were to follow him outside. (I—Greta—whose body Zeoker was using, was clad in a nightgown. Fortunately it was late in the evening.) Zeoker walked out the front door and looked down to the right, where on the slab deck sat a pot containing a large dead aloe plant. He gazed at the plant with the saddest expression imaginable. He even wiped away imaginary tears from each eye, as if weeping at the tragic death of the aloe. He waved his hand over the dead plant.

Dick asked if the plants could be brought back to life with care and attention. Zeoker shook his head. Sandy mumbled regrets for his negligence.

Zeoker's expression brightened considerably when he turned his attention to the plant next to it: a small cactus with a bright orange bloom on top. For some reason this struck him as funny, and he put his hand over his mouth in the typically Archan way of covering a laugh.

He then toured both the outside and inside of the house. He was amused by the bedspread, which had a monochromatic reproduction of a tree or shrub. As he passed through the living room, he saw Sandy and Goldie's daughters Vicki and Beth, sound asleep on the floor. Through sign language he communicated the statement that human beings when small are all pure and beautiful; it is only through the improper teachings of adults that their beauty and purity are corrupted.

Zeoker also examined the family's little pet poodle. He leaned over and stretched her out. The dog remained very still and uncharacteristically calm throughout this, making no objection.

A few minutes later, after further communication, Zeoker left. When that happened, we examined the sprig that he had given Goldie. We were astounded and bewildered to discover that it was made of plastic.

Then Tauri appeared and of course everybody immediately wanted to know what Zeoker had had in mind when he played this "trick." She responded with a question: "Do you know what the lesson is?"

"I'm afraid not," Goldie said, "but I would like to know."

Dick said, "I pass."

"The lesson is for all of you but perhaps most for my channel.

"Tonight you went to a beautiful place, did you not? And as you [Dick] said, you did not eat, you dined. You fed your human frames and enjoyed the beauty of the place, and the very quality of the food—then you went outside . . . do you remember what my channel said as she stood there waiting for the car?

"She commented first on the trees in front of this most beautiful building with its very careful cooking. And then she commented on how perfect and 'lovely, lovely' were the shrubs on either side.

"I think Zeoker's lesson is that you should not always look at things as they appear—because indeed they were all plastic. He is trying to say to you: 'Don't ever go by appearances,' no matter how 'lovely, lovely.' He subtly gives you all a lesson in observation—to look beneath what you think you see and always test, because you see, Dick, it's not just your voice and your music that you have to know to survive."

"It was so obvious," Dick said. "We saw it but we did not observe it."

"Oh, but my channel observed it as lovely. And she was wrong, wrong. And indeed, if you choose to take as the lesson the fact that you [Sandy] do not care for your own plants, that too would be accountable."

"It might also point out some of the plastic values we have here on our planet," Dick suggested.

"That's another way of looking at it," Tauri agreed. "Whereas the plants from Archa can last just so long in dense air, this one should remind you forevermore of a lesson that should not die. So, indeed, it becomes quite a 'lovely, lovely' gift to you."

(After our visit to Sandy and Goldie's, they called to tell us that recently and unaccountably the allegedly very dead aloe plant had sprouted new blooms! Dick asked Zeoker about this and was told, by signs and gestures, that the plant was indeed dead and that these blooms were not a product of the same root structure. They were a present from Zeoker to Sandy and Goldie. The tiny "dead" plant has grown and bred over these nine years. The stalks are now over twenty inches tall, but none of the offspring have stalks . . . just that parent plant. Sandy has taken well over a thousand offspring to his local nursery, and he has potted hundreds of babies to be given as special gifts to friends and neighbors.)

The lesson Zeoker gave us that memorable evening has expanded over time. Dick and I are most aware of how much the society in which we have been raised has shaped our thought and observation. We both know that ordinary awareness is dominated by the choices we are accustomed to making, by what we like and dislike. Others can have the same experience and observe it in a totally different manner. These differences in cultural patterns may be a large factor in the inability of man to get along with his fellow man. When the leaders of the world need translators to communicate with each other, the content of the message given may not be the content of the message received. These problems would disappear if communication were achieved telepathically; thoughts would be transmitted without the distortion of words.

We were back in Westport when we next encountered Zeoker. It was a couple of weeks later, late December evening, that he appeared in the middle of a conversation Dick and I were having with Ann. Zeoker shook hands with Dick, who then introduced him to Ann; she had not met him before.

Dick rushed off to the bedroom where Alan lay sleeping and brought him back, sleepy and befuddled. Zeoker took him back to the room so that Alan, home after a business trip, could resume the sleep state he had not entirely left. Then Zeoker returned to the living room and materialized a delicate-looking sprig from what everyone assumed was a shrub from Florida. Asked about this, Zeoker nodded. The sprig was intended as a gift for Ann.

Zeoker indicated that Ann should learn how to "heal" plants. He urged her to take a course in botany at Dartmouth, where she was studying.

He went over to the bookshelves in the hallway, apparently looking for a particular book and not finding it. He looked frustrated. He pointed to the space next to a volume entitled *Emerson's Essays* as the spot that the missing book had occupied. Dick explained that not long ago I had cleared out several hundred books and rearranged the shelves.

Ann recalled the book that had been there and asked Zeoker if he was looking for Henry David Thoreau's *Walden.* Zeoker lit up. Ann told him that she had written an essay on Thoreau when she was a senior in high school. Dick asked if Zeoker had worked with Thoreau and Zeoker nodded casual assent.

Dick, Ann, and Zeoker retired to Ann's bedroom to look for the essay on Thoreau. Ann thought it was probably at college, which subsequently proved correct. Meanwhile Zeoker was studying a plant on Ann's desk. He picked it up and did a pruning demonstration for Dick and Ann. He then walked to the bathroom, took some water in his hands, and showed how to properly water the plant and wash down its leaves.

Zeoker led the party into Jill's room, where an ailing plant that Ann had brought home from school was sitting on the west window. Zeoker took it out of its pot and gave Dick and Ann another pruning demonstration. In the bathroom he moisturized the leaves and roots, then staked the plant with Q-tips. He indicated that we should leave it staked in this manner for "one moon" (a month); then we could remove the stakes.

Zeoker let Ann know that a proper "love energy" from her to the plant would significantly improve its growth and well-being.

That was Zeoker's final message. When he left, Dick and Ann told me about his visit. Ann put the shrub Zeoker had given her on the living-room table and we resumed the conversation we had been having before his unexpected appearance.

A few minutes later we decided to retire for the night. Ann turned to pick up her shrub, only to discover that it was gone. We all searched the room to no avail. Ann was disappointed and upset. Then I remembered similar episodes in the past. I suggested that we go to Ann's room.

We did—and there it was, right in front of the pillow on her bed. It was a sweet good-night present to Ann. The scent of firna filled her room . . .

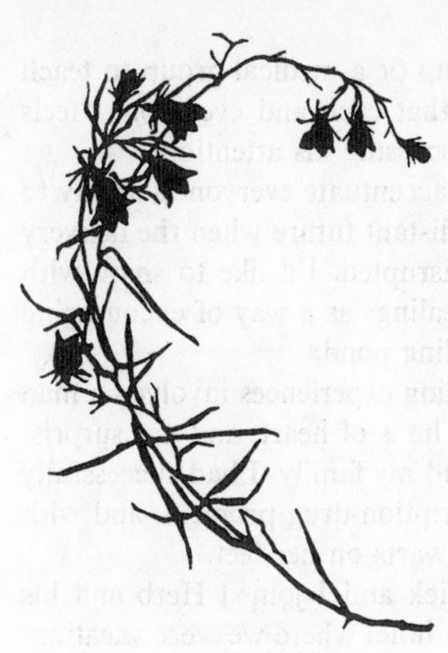

16

METAL BENDINGS and teleportations were not the only new phenomena occurring around us. There were—perhaps most important of all—healings.

The dictionary defines healing as the method we use "to make sound . . . to make whole . . . to restore wholeness." That is what healing is about: making a person whole. Healing can, does, and must deal simultaneously with the body, the mind, and the emotions. It also deals with the life force itself. It deals with the contents of the person's life, his reason for living and his way of living. And it deals with Earth energies and a person's ability to tap into them. Healing deals with you and it deals with me because everyone hurts and no one exists outside the laws of change.

Healing is the ability to summon up the good Earth energy at 7.83 Hz., or cycles per second—the "alpha frequency"—and pass it along to a needy individual. It was the frequency of the Earth when mankind evolved, and it is the frequency at which the self-healing abilities of the body are most stimulated. All of us are capable of drawing up this healing Earth energy and passing it along. Whether I have a lay group or a medical group to teach how to pass this energy, I find that each and every one "feels something" very quickly when focussing his attention.

The Ogattans encourage us to accentuate everyone's ability to heal, for the time in the not-too-distant future when the delivery of "normal" health services is disrupted. I'd like to share with you a few stories of successful healings as a way of encouraging you to put your toe into the healing pond.

One of my most treasured healing experiences involved a man named Herb, as large of girth as he is of heart, and not surprisingly dubbed "Buddha" by me and my family. I had successfully worked with his wife on a prescription-drug problem, and with his daughter, who suffered from warts on her feet.

On this particular morning Dick and I joined Herb and his wife for breakfast in his suite at a hotel where we were vacationing together for a weekend of fun. The waiter wheeled in a lavish spread; he laid it all out and proceeded to pour the steaming hot coffee into our cups. As he approached Herb, he tripped on the carpet's edge, and the scalding coffee streamed over Herb's hand and forearm. Herb howled in agony and doubled over as Dick, Karen, and I froze in horror. Instinctively Karen jumped up and ran to the phone to call for the house doctor. Dick turned quietly to me and simply murmured, "You're a healer. Can you do something?"

I looked at poor Herb questioningly and he nodded assent. Karen returned to the table and sat down. I ran into the bathroom, washed, and came back to our Buddha whose burned skin looked horrible: bright, red, shiny, starting to pucker. Closing my eyes, I put my hands two or three inches over the burns.

Herb recalled, "As she passed her hands over my arm and hand, my heart stopped thudding. My breathing became more regular, easier, and a sort of peace came over me. 'Close your eyes,' she whispered. I did. Everything felt cool. And then the pain was gone!

"I opened my eyes and stared at my hand and forearm, which were as normal looking as they had been before breakfast not five minutes earlier. No redness, no shine, no blistering, no pain!

"There were tears in everybody's eyes, even mine. Karen said that Greta had passed her hands over me a few times, Dick sitting behind her, 'pushing energy' to her.

"I don't pretend to know what Greta did, but for me it was plainly and simply a miracle. When it happens to you, it is a very different ball game than when it happens to somebody else. I'm not into all the things she is into, but I'll tell you this: She is a genuine healer and a very special lady."

This was a typical healing session for me: brief, with a feeling of balance and control. It isn't always that way. Now and then one or more of the Ogatta group come through and use me as their channel for healing. They use these occasions to instruct those present and to generate energy beyond my earthly skills.

One of the first such episodes involved a friend of a friend, Clarence, a man who was grossly overweight before he underwent a short-circuit stomach by-pass operation. In time his weight went down to two hundred and sixty pounds. Unfortunately, as all this was happening, his legs turned black from the knees down. Doctors decreed the situation hopeless. They would have to amputate, they said. Meanwhile, Clarence suffered from constant pain and made it through the day only by massive ingestion of painkilling drugs and shots. Eldon Byrd, our mutual acquaintance, told Dick and me that Clarence had come to the end of his rope.

Before we met with Clarence, we talked with two doctors who told us he should never have had that sort of purely cosmetic operation in the first place. They agreed that amputation was inescapable. Still, Clarence was refusing to have that done.

On a blustery December day in 1977, at one-thirty in the afternoon, he, his wife and Eldon Byrd arrived at our place. Clarence was in a notably gloomy mood, evidently not particularly confident that we could do anything for him.

Ann took him into the living room and set him up on the massage table. Then Ann joined me, Dick, my brother Michael, Alan, Jonathan, and Clarence's wife in the bedroom, where I outlined where each of them was to stand in relation to the supine Clarence. Michael was to be at his feet, using a foot-reflexology method he had been studying for some time. Alan would be at the head, Ann and Jonathan on one side, and I on the other. Dick would stand behind me "power-packing," drawing up Earth energy and directing it to me, making me a doubly powerful vehicle for healing.

That arranged, we went into the living room and positioned ourselves around Clarence. We were about to start when suddenly Cjork took control. She asked "the little Oshanian" (Ann) to take Alan's position at Clarence's head and Alan to take hers at the side. The healing session that followed lasted twenty-five minutes.

Cjork was in charge all the way through, but she briefly surrendered the channel to others, including an entity that did not identify itself but who made a karate-like gesture. It was intended, apparently, to send charges of healing energy into Clarence. Tauri momentarily appeared, then made way for Bilakka, the master musician from Archa, who played "healing music" on the piano through my untrained hands.

Afterward Alan and Dick swore they had seen Cjork practice psychic surgery. In psychic surgery the healer's hands seem to penetrate the flesh of the patient, actually reaching inside the body to touch or remove a diseased part. When the hand is removed, the flesh is whole, betraying no evidence of penetration. Alan and Dick were certain they had seen Cjork's (my) right forefinger enter Clarence's skull.

All the while the healing was going on, Cjork gave lessons in healing. At one point she had Ann get a tape measure, then used it to determine the length of the viscerated scar on Clarence's stomach. It was exactly eleven inches long. She then directed everybody to "explode" with energy and send it to all parts of Clarence's body.

Thirty-two seconds later—Cjork noted the exact time—the scar was measured again. It was now three-quarters-of-an-inch longer than it had been half a minute ago. She would not explain what this meant, offering only the cryptic remark that we would know about it in the future, when we had progressed further.

Cjork continued her work on all parts of the body. She had

Clarence exhale loudly at certain times. At other times Clarence seemed to leave his body under Cjork's direction.

Finally Cjork departed and Clarence got up. "I haven't felt this relaxed in five years," he said. "I can't believe it. I'm totally free of pain."

While it was only 2:15 P.M., I insisted that Clarence stay for another three hours. I wanted assurance that this was not just a momentary effect. In fact, as time passed, he seemed to feel better and better. At last, when he got up to go, he bounded to his feet, cheerfully donned his coat, and happily walked out into a brewing blizzard.

I talked with Clarence a couple of nights later. He said he was "incredibly relaxed and free of any pain whatsoever." This was the "experience of his life," he told me. His calves and feet were turning back into the normal pink color of healthy flesh, and the stinging sensation that had afflicted his thigh for so long had entirely vanished.

"I just can't fathom how these things happen," he said.

We lost touch with Clarence the next year, but at that time he was still pain-free.

Healings continued to happen. Another took place in an apartment in New York City a few days later, when we worked on a man who had a malignant prostate tumor. During this (successful) healing Zeoker assumed the channel and materialized a leaf, which he placed on the prostate. An anonymous entity appeared to participate, and finally Cjork came through to complete the process. At the end of the healing a spoon I had placed on a nearby mantle bent dramatically in full view of everyone.

After the man was proclaimed well by his physician (who had no explanation for the cure), the patient asked me if there was anything at all that he could do for me since I never take payment for healings. "Yes," I told him with a straight face. "Please stop telling people that you were cured of your prostate problems through a laying-on of hands!"

That June, while we were visiting Andrija in his Ossining laboratory, I asked him to look at Dick's left eye because a capillary had broken and left it bloodshot. Andrija examined it and had just said it wasn't serious when Cjork abruptly entered the channel and said, "It may be nothing for you humans but for me it's very easy to bring something to help it." At that moment a small white bottle materialized in my right hand.

Andrija tasted it, sniffed it, and looked it over carefully. He concluded that the bottle, which had no prescription number or any other kind of identification, contained Opthalmic solution for the eye. Oddly, the bottle seemed to have been used; the evidence was a dirty cap. Andrija removed the cap and placed it on the table beside him.

He put some of the solution in Dick's eye, then reached for the cap, intending to put it back on the bottle. But it was nowhere to be found.

By this time Cjork was gone and I was able to join Dick and Andrija in the search for the missing cap. Meanwhile Dick's eye was noticeably improving.

Finally, after we had given up trying to find the cap, Andrija told us we could save the solution if we blocked the opening with a toothpick. As he spoke, the cap materialized in exactly the same spot from which it had disappeared. Within half an hour Dick's eye redness was completely gone.

To me healing is one of the most exciting manifestations of the paranormal. It is a visible experience in which I participate with another human being (and with Dick, who acts as an energy-booster, a "power pack") and can see some immediate results. When a person is able to "touch" another person, it is a moving and emotional experience.

Unfortunately, some healing sessions do not elicit the anticipated results. I think of one particular case involving a woman who was not only a pediatrician but a psychiatrist as well. She had gone to a prestigious medical school for a residency to earn the latter specialty degree, and we stood in awe of this academic achievement made in mid-life. We soon discovered that she had rheumatoid arthritis and her hands could no longer safely support the babies whom she held in her work. This is what sent her back for the second residency.

At the time we met her, she admitted that she had been to the finest doctors in the country; indeed, living in a major city in the Northeast and being on the staff of its most prestigious hospital, she had access to the best advice and treatment possible. All this, however, was to no avail; she was growing steadily worse.

She couldn't open a bottle of tonic water without first propping her arms up at the elbows and using a mechanical device to pop the top. One hand was badly curled. She did her best to conceal it, but the sight was not pretty and the hand was not operative. I agreed to try to help her while I was in her hometown lecturing at a college. I imposed one small condition: Would she please write up the experience if it were a success so that I could have it in my file. She assured me that that was no problem. She understood that some day in the future I might want to use the data to help someone else with the same ailment.

I worked with her, hands on, twice at her home, and then by remote, every Wednesday evening for six weeks. Her hand grew increasingly stronger and she measured the strength daily with the use of her sphygmomanometer (blood-pressure gauge). Each time, I'd ask if she was writing it down and she said she was, "in detail." In truth, she never wrote a word.

Suspecting as much, I once asked her to send me what she had to date and she replied, "Oh, it's all on a yellow legal pad. I'll transcribe it over to my medical stationery at the end." This was a woman who never hesitated to call me at all hours of the day and night with questions, demands, and excited claims of her progress and cure. She said, "None of those famous doctors at the hospital have been able to do for me what you have done!"

The healing sessions tapered off and we insisted that she fulfill her promise and commit to paper the results for our file. The hedging began with "Well, you know I took gold shots a few months ago, and this could be a factor in my regression." Soon we were hearing, "Oh, I've been on a new diet and that is one of the possibilities in my cure." Finally: "You know, I don't think my colleagues would appreciate or understand my sanctioning healing, since we don't have any proof positive."

We terminated the healings (although her calls continued for a while). Sad to relate, in three months' time she was right back where she had started, her hand curled and weak. Some healing does not hold and some people invite recurrences or substitute illnesses.

It is sadly true that being a healer and going one-on-one with an individual reduces the effectiveness that I can achieve in scribing the pen and trumpeting the word, the job I signed on to do with the Ogatta group. When I broached this conflict to Dick, his reply was comforting: "If you had wanted to be a healer, you would have gone to medical school and devoted your life to healing the sick. In the realm of the paranormal, healing is only one of the manifestations that are exhibited through you, albeit the one that gives you the greatest personal satisfaction. Unfortunately, you can't satisfy all of your desires or requests in this area or you won't have time for the job at hand."

There are those people who want their illness; who need their illness; who depend on their illness; who don't want to lose their illness. It is their major topic of conversation. It serves to keep the family tied to them. It is satisfying to them in a sad but real way. Such persons are not candidates for healing and you can spot them with relative ease. Healing is not for everyone, and people should ask for healing; it shouldn't be volunteered. There are exceptions, of course. Then, too, there are two answers to the question: yes or no. There are times one must say no. I have learned to exercise this right without guilt.

We have incorporated into our seminars, workshops, and conferences, however, an experience for the attendees that teaches how to manifest a "healing energy." All of us are capable of doing it. All of us can help ourselves and others, should the occasion arise.

Another healing experience involved the president of Sonesta International Hotels Corporation, Roger Sonnabend. He came to our home in 1982 complaining of a sore shoulder. On seeing him, however, I was compelled to ask about his face, which was rather lopsided. He quietly told me that he had had Bell's palsy more than fifteen years earlier and it left him with a "droop to the eye and mouth." He said one consequence was that he could neither wink nor whistle.

After working on him for a few moments, I asked him, "What was it you said you couldn't do?"

"Wink or whistle," he said.

"Try," I suggested.

He could do both. He was so astounded that he didn't realize immediately that his face had "lifted" and no longer drooped. When he saw his wife crying, he went to the mirror in the hall and looked at himself. "My goodness!" was all he could manage before he, too, was overwhelmed with emotion. He became an instant believer, and along with his beautiful wife, a strong and continuing supporter of our work.

This is the story in his own words:

> Our visit on August 22 was intended to be a purely social one. Joan and I had heard about you from Hans Keller, one of your great Swiss admirers, whose knee you had cured, and Elmer Capoolse of Egypt whose back you healed. As we were driving from Boston to New York, the opportunity to visit was one we couldn't resist.
>
> After a few minutes of social conversation, Greta asked about my face because the "field" about me was so lopsided.
>
> I told her about my incomplete recovery from Bell's palsy in 1967. She graciously treated my face and within a few minutes a remarkable transformation took place. Looking in the mirror, I discovered the right side of my face that drooped so much had raised significantly and was much in balance with the left side. Remarkably, for the first time in sixteen or so years, I could comfortably and easily wink my right eye and whistle, something I had not been able to do because I could not bring my lips into the appropriate position to whistle.
>
> As the result of a second visit and treatment on September 11, my face very quickly straightened out even further so that my smile is now a completely balanced one, and I can whistle more easily than before. As I write this, my improved condition has remained. Greta's encouragement to think positively certainly is contributing to my maintaining the benefits achieved with her.
>
> During my first session I experienced heat and energy penetrating my face, and after the treatment my face felt very different than before, almost as though a restriction had been lifted from the muscles on the right side. In the second treatment, I did not experience

the same degree of heat, but was aware of energy entering my face. Subsequently, the treated right side of my face felt very different than it had before, and quite different from the left side. It felt more relaxed.

I am ecstatic with my experience and feel deeply indebted. This very pragmatic businessman is now a believer!

There are hundreds of healing stories. There are dozens of letters. Not everyone is as willing to commit to paper his experience after the fact. One of my favorite episodes concerns a lovely young woman named Sasha. Sasha arrived at our S.T.A.R. House in October 1985 in a wheelchair and back brace. Her letter tells her story better than I can:

Dearest Greta—

I came to you on a Friday afternoon, after having traveled by wheelchair and airplane, wearing a back support and managing to carry only a tiny purse. My bag was carried for me.

For month after month I had been experiencing excruciating pain in my groin, thigh, leg, and foot. My problems began with numbness in my foot. The numbness traveled upward and partial paralysis came next; then the spasms and the pain. It became impossible for me to walk down the street.

I had tried acupuncture, which I had experienced successfully many times in the past, but it no longer worked for me. I went to a chiropractor, who yanked and pulled and stretched, and used ultrasound and other machines. I had a CAT scan which clearly showed two discs bulging and pressing against my spinal cord, which of course kept my sciatic nerve and surrounding nerves screaming all the time (that huge lump that you felt).

I had a sudden flash and I knew that it wasn't just my body that needed repair—it was body, soul, spirit, and mind that needed healing. When I realized this, I decided to call you. I knew, of course, that you had healed a close friend of mine with a serious shoulder and arm problem.

When I told the neurologist that I was going to see you, I

was shocked and delighted that he supported my decision, because this very famous and supposedly conservative doctor no longer had any answers for me.

The moment I met you, I knew I was "home." I knew from your eyes and your vibes that something wonderful would happen. I of course could never have imagined the extent, the total transformation from "sickness" to "wellness" that I would undergo.

Your first healing took away that wretched spasm. That healing and subsequent healings, combined with the sensations of love, warmth, calm, the vibrations going through my body, and the feeling of inward cleansing, brought me an incredible feeling of peacefulness. I was crying and laughing all at the same time.

I experienced the greatest highs with you. If I had walked into a dark room, my inward glow would have lighted the way.

I left my apartment and came to you struggling physically and scattered psychologically and emotionally. An entirely different person left on that Sunday afternoon—a healed, whole person. I arrived a disaster and left a miracle.

No words can express what I feel, so I'll say simply that I am grateful for your gift—and I love you!

SASHA

At this writing, almost two years later, Sasha has taken a flat in Paris and dashes all around France in her high heels. In her visit to S.T.A.R. House in November 1987, Sasha walked all over the mountain with Dick and me. She was the picture of health. One would never connect this vibrant woman with the broken doll who came here only two short years ago.

A week seldom passes that I am not involved in healing. I view each session as an opportunity to exchange energies with someone. I rejoice when there is success and I grieve when there is not, but I never feel elation or guilt. I am only a channel through whom energies flow. Indeed, if the healing can be likened to a lamp, the patient is the light bulb and I am merely the cord.

Healing is a subject that concerns every one of us. Few subjects are so all-encompassing.

The larger issue of becoming healthy revolves around the willingness to accept responsibility for illness and to explore those aspects that defy personal wholeness.

Healing is hardly a new subject. Virtually every past civilization known to man regarded healing as a symbol of profound significance and prominently recorded it. Illness was seen as a consequence of falling out of harmony with nature. Healing involved a restoration of balance, a reconciliation between man and the forces that govern life. All the myths, stories, and fables that have come down to us are filled with the wonderment of great healings. The ancient Greek, Indian, and Chinese cultures shared the conviction that healings could not be tackled on a physical level alone. Man was a multidimensional being, a whole being consisting of body, mind, and spirit. Holism represents the integration of physiology, psychology, and spirituality—the synthesis of human life.

Five centuries before the greatest healer of the Common Era, Jesus Christ, Indian texts described techniques for channeling the vital energy—they called it "prana"—to cure the sick. The energy was transferred by the healer's touch and by the mind. The Chinese used the notion that energy flows through the mysterious pathways of the body and that disease occurs when the energy in these pathways is blocked and diverted. They treated health problems by stimulating and unblocking the energy flow. Today we call it "passing energy." It is something everyone can do.

Hippocrates, the father of modern medicine, studied the entire patient and dealt extensively with the patient's diet and his environment, both mental and physical. One of his more interesting books, *Air, Water, and Places,* written around the turn of the fifth century B.C., could be classed as a treatise on human ecology dealing with the "whole man." One passage tallies with what healers of all ages have described: "The heat that oozes out of the hand, on being applied to the sick, is highly salutary. It has often appeared while I have been soothing my patients, as if there was a singular property in my hands to pull and draw away from the affected parts any aches and diverse impurities. This occurs when laying my hand upon the affected place."

With the rise of scientific medicine in Greece, Plato chided physicians in his *Dialogues:* "If the head and body are to be well, you must begin by curing the soul. The great error in our day in the treatment of the human body is that the physicians separate the soul from the body." The Gospels record twenty-six individual healings and twenty-seven group healings by Jesus, along with nine multiple healings by His apostles. The methods that were used were touch, words, prayers, faith, and natural compassion.

All over the world, whatever the religious context, there is evidence that high spiritual attainment is often accompanied by the power to heal. But healing abilities do not require spiritual enlightenment. Healing does not even imply enlightenment. Healing energy, like physical energy, is devoid of an inherent value system. It can be used as the person directing it desires. I am not saying that you can generate healing without a positive thrust! Egotism and the desire for personal glory block the activation of healing energy.

Healing has come full cycle and is enjoying a resurgence. Healing does not stand opposed to modern medicine. Healing goes along with, not in place of, modern medicine. Medical orthodoxy specializes in disease invasion, not health. It concerns itself with crisis intervention and diseased parts, not the whole person. We find ourselves in a world of specialists. The original doctors were healer-priests. Back then, treatment was to exorcise the "evil spirits" with incantations and exorcising rituals . . . elixirs . . . vapors. Things have not changed that much. What they called "evil spirits" then, they now call "disease entities." Today medicine focusses on exorcising these "disease entities" and not paying too much attention to the person that is *housing* the "evil spirit/disease entity."

Healing cannot be understood in reductionist terms alone. The analyzing of the part does not always allow for understanding the cause of the illness, and medicating the ailing part treats the effect but many times does nothing to eliminate the cause. Personality and behavioral traits are known to play a significant part in predisposing people to certain diseases. Deep disappointment, repressed emotions, grief, guilt, and fear all contribute mightily to illness. "Fear of the unknown" is a constant theme of mankind, laments the Ogatta group. Fear's thread is woven into the fabric of human history.

I am reminded of an old Arab tale telling of a caravan that met Pestilence on the way to Baghdad. "Why must you hasten to Baghdad?" asked the Arab chieftain. "To claim five thousand lives," Pestilence replied. Later, when the chieftain again encountered Pestilence, he shouted, "You lied to me! Instead of five thousand lives you took fifty thousand!" "Nay," Pestilence said. "I took not one more or one less than five thousand. It was *fear* that killed the rest."

We have all come to delegate responsibility for our health to the doctor and his drugs rather than examine life-styles and unhealthy behavior. We prefer to be told that we suffer from stress and hypertension rather than change our overcompetitive environment. We use medical diagnosis as a cover-up for social problems, and we use illness to solve personal problems.

The point is that everyone participates in his or her health or illness at all times. The concept of individual choice is central to holistic healing. The patient is an active and responsible participant in the healing process rather than a passive "victim" of either the disease or the treatment.

William Tiller of Stanford University says, "Each cell and gland in our body has a characteristic frequency at which it will absorb and emit EM radiations. When the gland or organ does not absorb and transmit its characteristic frequency, it is not sending its proper electromagnetic message. Disease is the result."

The Ogatta group put it another way. They taught us that healing is really a "harmonizing of energies." They explained that "parts of the body communicate with each other on narrow bands or wavelengths"; and that the body becomes 'dis-eased' "when communication between these parts is disrupted." They likened the process to having a message beamed on one channel while you are tuned to another channel. The message goes out but "there is nobody 'home' to receive it."

We read that the earth energy of 7.83 Hz. is the harmonizing frequency that allows the body to return to its proper bands or wavelengths on which it can communicate. The Ogatta group gave meaning in lay language to how the healing process works.

Healing is putting the part back into its proper frequency, enabling it to play its role in the functioning of the body. A healer is a person who is adaptable as a conductor between the Earth energy all around us and the person with a malfunctioning gland or organ, the patient. Somewhere, sometime, every one of us has eased another's distress—his 'dis-ease.' We know the power is in us.

I believe we are all potential healers. It is time to take a holistic view of our health. We cannot abdicate to physicians the responsibility of returning us to wellness, when our mental state and life-style bring us to illness.

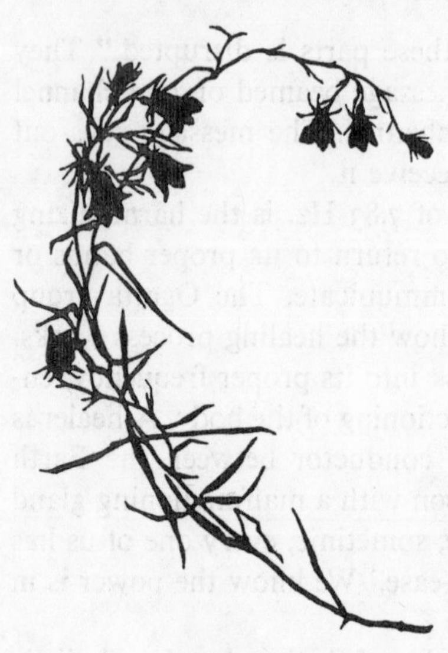

17

THERE WAS A TIME that I was regularly experiencing something a bit disconcerting for all concerned: spontaneous regressions back into my childhood, to the days when I first met the Ogattans and traveled "on the rainbow" with them. I returned to a number of different ages, from about three to eighteen, and I relived a variety of different events, not all of them having to do with my extraterrestrial friends.

One aspect that came through repeatedly was my sense, even then, that something important was happening to me—something I must not communicate with others.

"I know things that other people don't know," I said in a seven-year-old's voice. "I can't tell them, though. They'll think I'm odd. I used to tell them some of the things I did and saw. They said I had a 'vivid imagination.' So I don't tell them anymore.

"Sometimes I go out there on the rainbow. I ride way out there —on the color blue. I hear beautiful music and see beautiful colors. You may not believe this but sometimes I see the music and hear the colors.

"The stars in the sky—they look like balloons going by. I see glass trees that you can see through, lots of them. They're beautiful.

"An island is going to pop right out of the water—in the 'seas that are south' on Earth. I know it's going to happen. Lots of land is going to come out of the water and lots of land is going to fall into the water. I can see that. But not for a long time. Not for more than fifty years! I'll be an old lady then. I can't tell anybody this. They'll think I'm an odd child. So I keep it to myself.

"The sad part is that I won't be able to do this much longer. I don't know why I can't stay out there on the rainbow and never come back. But I always end up back here, in my bed, even though I'd rather stay out there forever and never come back.

"I won't be doing this much longer. And I won't have any memory of it anymore. I know! I know! They'll wipe my memory and I won't remember anything. I know! I know! It's very sad for me!"

Not too many years ago I picked up a wonderful little book, *Mister God, This Is Anna.* In it, four-year-old Anna seems to understand with absolute certainty the purpose of being, the essence of feeling, the meaning of love. She finds God in her "middle." I read that with a rush of emotion which literally took my breath away.

In a prior regression (fortunately taped) to my own four-year-old childhood through the ministrations of the Ogatta group, I came back to that experience. "Young Greta" had also touched those present on that occasion in their "middles." The transcript of the experience follows:

YOUNG GRETA: I can talk to flowers, you know. Can you?

DICK: Sometimes. Not all the time. Can you talk to this rose?

YOUNG GRETA: You can talk to any flower. It isn't just the rose you can talk to. The flowers that don't have one flap over the other, like . . . like the pansies . . . they don't . . . they don't . . .

DICK: Communicate? Talk back?

YOUNG GRETA: Yes, they don't "communicate" very well because they are flat. They don't have a [points to her navel].

DICK: A center?

YOUNG GRETA: A center. So when you have a flower like a rose or a tulip or flowers that have a lot of flaps [petals] and they hold the wet [moisture] . . . then it's easy to talk to them. It's harder to talk to the flowers that are flat. Also, they don't have the pretty smell. They can't hold in *in their middle* . . . and in their middle is where all their life and energy is. That's right! I know that. But not many big people know that.

DICK: How do you talk with them? Do you use words or do you just think words?

YOUNG GRETA: Sometimes both. I'll tell you a secret. If you put your hands under your belly button and you close your eyes and then you push out all your thoughts into them . . . they'll open right up and answer if you listen.

DICK: Yes! And with a very sweet musical voice!

YOUNG GRETA: Uh huh. Because almost everything that you can see and that you can touch *you can hear.* But most big people just don't listen to hear it at all. And that's very sad.

Dick always found these interludes with "young Greta," as he called her, stimulating, exciting, and fun. He said he was the only man on Earth who could go back and converse with his wife as she was in her childhood. And there were many hilarious moments—for Dick, that is. What other man has seen his fifty-seven-year-old wife acrobatically tossing a leg up and around her neck? Or tap dancing as she "shuffles off to Buffalo"? "I couldn't! I didn't!" I'd protest afterward. "You did!" he'd insist as he doubled over in amusement. There are times I think he loves Young Greta more than he does this far less flamboyant Greta, however much he denies it. "Oh, Gret," he'd say, "you have to see her and hear her when that high-pitched little voice tells me, 'I hate freckles! I hate beets!' "

Let's consider that "high-pitched little voice" for a moment. When I was in my teens, I suffered a horseback riding accident. One of my vocal cords was permanently damaged. It wasn't really a problem except that I could no longer get into the upper ranges. My voice is low pitched and husky. *But,* when I am in regression with the Ogatta group, those high notes are *there!* When the Ogattans use me as a channel, my voice takes on all manner of ranges! When the Tchauvians sing through me, they sing in multiple-voice *harmony* in notes I cannot reach. Incredible!

During one particularly interesting young Greta session with my husband and son, the subject of "little beings" came up. Tauri entered the channel after a little while and gave us all something to think about. She said, "You humans must learn in the very near future to 'hook in' to other dimensions. When you do, you will see things you never saw before and you will wonder why this is so. It's like Buckminster Fuller when he talked about ultraviolet and infrared. Your technology can pick up what your eyes cannot.

"Now, you know that those rays are there, don't you? If only, when you are out in your gardens, you opened your eyes, you would literally see physical remnants left by beings you choose to call devas, fairies, little people. Don't you think that a plant has feelings? With whom do they communicate? Another plant, of course. Who makes the marriage? How about little beings? Some you can see . . . like bees. Some you do not see. One of your jobs on this planet is to be sure you become aware of all there is to see in the gardens. And if you choose to call them fairies or devas, it matters not. No, it doesn't matter what you call them. What matters is that they are there!"

But these sessions were not all fun and games, as Tauri was to tell us. They served two very distinct purposes. First, they brought into the present—for me—the experiences I had shared with the Ogatta group in my younger days. And second (and Tauri said, more important), it gave Dick an insight into the inner workings of my mind and its functioning so that he could better serve as a total support system as we went forward in the work.

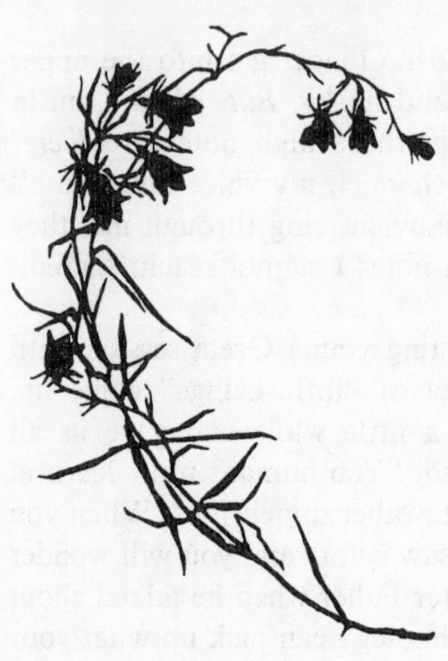

18

ONE EVENING in July of 1979, Dick, Alan, and I were watching a television movie, *A Fire in the Sky,* about a comet that collides with Phoenix, Arizona. Two hours into the movie, I got up to go to the bathroom. Dick recalled:

"Alan and I . . . heard what we thought was something dropping on the floor. We bolted into the office to see if Greta was all right. She was *gone*—no place in sight.

"Alan and I knew that she couldn't have gotten from the bathroom to any other place in the house without first passing one of us. She was not in the office, the bathroom, or Alan's room. She had not gone downstairs, because we would have heard her on the stairs. We searched the house thoroughly, however. All of the lights were turned on and all of the closets thrown open. We made a complete tour through the house and then repeated the process. *Greta was not in the house!*

"We were about to start a third pass through the house when Alan called me into the office. Greta lay crumpled on the floor on her stomach, completely passed out. I was kneeling over her when the phone rang. It was Greta's youngest brother phoning to tell us that Andrija had just called him from Canada.

"I hurriedly told him what had happened, that Greta had been dematerialized and rematerialized, and asked him for the number to reach Andrija. I wanted him to give me a quick review of the procedures to use under these circumstances to minimize the shock to Greta's system. I placed the call and was told that they would have to locate Dr. Puharich and have him return the call.

"It took approximately twenty minutes for Andrija to return the call. During that time Greta came in and out in a very disoriented way. She was attempting to communicate something to us, although she was stammering badly, getting hung up on the word *'not.'* She was stammering, 'Not . . . not . . . not . . . not . . . not . . . not . . .' and finally, a very weak and very confused and fuzzy 'not . . . not make-believe.' Then, back out.

"Andrija called and I explained the purpose of my call to him. I asked him to review the procedures to use for Greta's health. The consequences of a dematerialization on a human can be dire if not handled properly. Andrija refreshed my memory. I had already gotten a small glass of milk to counteract the hydrochloric acidity to the stomach; that I had remembered. He suggested slow steady hand-passes from the top of the head to the feet without touching the body, this to soothe and calm a disoriented bioplasmic body.

"Shortly after this call Greta became confusedly awake and worked her way down to the bedroom. I say 'worked' because she was not aware of Alan or me and crawled from the office to the stairs and then down the stairs. Alan was directly in front of her to assist her descent, but she insisted on doing it herself. At the stairs she turned backward and backed down the stairs on all fours.

"She got onto the bed in her dazed state. Alan and I continued the hand-passes over her. From time to time she would appear to come back to a conscious state, during which time she commented on how good the 'massage' felt . . .

"Greta expressed the following thoughts in her disoriented

state. She was not aware of having expressed them when she became fully conscious and normally awake.

"There was nothing that we could do to prevent the entry of this fireball to the earth. There would be lots of fire and many would die. The fireball was a comet. It would hit at a place that she had never been, but she thought it was the United States.

"She didn't see the entities that showed her this real 'fireball' but she heard their voices. They said that since there was nothing anyone could do to prevent its destruction on the Earth there was *no reason for Greta to continue to write and speak out.* The entities were *not* from the Ogatta group. They dematerialized her as she reached for the door in the bathroom to leave.

"When we found Greta crumpled on the floor of the office, she said, 'They dropped me on my knees. They dropped me on my knees.' This is a very tender spot at the moment from a previous fall and this return on the knees caused Greta a great deal of pain . . .

"Alan went back upstairs at approximately 1:00 A.M. Greta went to sleep. I continued to watch her for a period of time until I felt that she would be able to pass the night uneventfully."

A week later Tauri appeared with some explanations for what had been a most upsetting experience for all of us. She asked Dick, "Do you remember meeting Kari-on?"

The name meant nothing to Dick.

"You remember Thornis? You also remember the fact that it was Thornis who was in the channel the last time Greta was taken? He was the one who saved our channel from any harm, and I owed him one. I told you that those from Lathea have a very advanced technology, like ours, and while they would not do anything to harm planet Earth, they are not in favor of our helping Earth in its transition.

"After the incident with Thornis offering the 'one with holes in his face' [Alan] the powers of materialization and dematerialization, they agreed not to interfere with our channels. We never interfere with their channels."

"I didn't know they had channels here on Earth!" Dick said, surprised.

"They have channels, but not on Earth. Anyway, our channel was lying in her usual place watching your wondrous machine about a 'comet' that would hit the Earth. Kari-on thought this would be a marvelous time to show our channel the 'real' comet that will hit your planet in the future. I was there when he took her. There was no permanent harm that could happen to our channel, not that I could have stopped Kari-on from taking her. She told you some of it, but not all of it. We had shown the channel this before when she saw the future of planet Earth. There is nothing that can be done to prevent this 'comet' from striking the Earth.

"Kari-on tried to use this information to tell Greta that, since nothing could be done about this destruction, there was no purpose in her 'scribing the pen and trumpeting the voice.' He started to tell her the details of time and location, but I blocked this information. It is a terrible thing to be saddled with information about which you can do nothing but brood. Do you remember the lady who predicted your father's graduation [death] and the unfair burden it placed upon the channel?

"There is no need to possess information about which there is nothing you can do. We of the Ogatta group do not burden anyone with this type of information and so I blocked it when Kari-on started to give it to our channel. Hence, the confused and stammered answer when you questioned the time and place.

"Now we are even. I no longer 'owe' the Latheans anything. I am not very happy with what they did. Thornis said that they would not interfere with our channels anymore. He didn't—but Kari-on did. They will hear about this in the higher Lathean tribunals."

Dick remarked, "It sounds to me as if what they did was morally wrong, after their understanding with you."

"It was much worse than morally wrong," Tauri replied. "I won't forget it. They didn't intentionally drop our channel back on her knees. That was just a bad reentry."

It was not the last such experience, unfortunately. Here is Dick's account of an event that occurred a few weeks later:

"We were preparing for bed and I had gone into the bathroom

and was brushing my teeth. Greta was in bed waiting for me—or so she had been when I entered the bathroom. I turned around to check, as has become my habit, and she was gone. I had not heard her leave, nor did I hear footsteps in any other part of the house.

"I checked around the downstairs hurriedly. No lights were on and I put them all on as I went. The lights in the yoga room were not on, nor were the lights on the stairs leading up. I turned the stair lights on and sprinted upstairs, calling Greta's name. I threw the lights on in the west wing of the house, then the living room. Since there were no lights on in the kitchen or dining room, I looked in quickly but returned to the west wing. *Nothing!*

"Down the stairs I went two steps at a time for another check. Again, *nothing*. Unfortunately nobody else was in the house at the time, so I couldn't call to get additional coverage for the search. I went back up the stairs—and found Greta in a heap in between the middle bedroom and the back (south) bedroom. She was lying with her legs bent under her, leaning against the east wall—but not in a waking state.

"I got to the floor and cradled her in my arms, holding her tightly and supporting her upper body. When I did this, a disoriented Greta, not in this time dimension, started speaking.

" 'Get Dickie. He can tell you what I couldn't say the last time.' 'Not—not—not—not—' 'Get Dickie. He knows.'

"This went on for some minutes. She was searching for the words 'not make believe,' which was the phrase that she had tried to relate to us when she was dropped back on her knees in the den from the last dematerialization that Kari-on of Lathea took her on . . . It was evident that she had been 'taken'—I knew not how but I suspected another dematerialization—to be shown either the same catastrophic scene or another like it.

"The calling for Dickie to give the missing words went on for some period, perhaps fifteen minutes, with the missing words being given but not 'heard' in whatever time frame she was asking from. A dryness came to her mouth and she asked for ice. There was nobody else in the house and I certainly was not going to get the ice with her not fully back on this plane and in control of the channel.

"Shortly after, Greta insisted on getting down to the bedroom. I tried to assist her but she waved me off, turned backward, and bumped her way down the stairs. I stayed right in front of her and kept the pace down the stairs to a very slow and controlled speed.

"When she got to the bottom of the landing, we were able to steady her on her feet and get her into bed. She called again and again for ice. Although I was sponging her face and letting the water drip into her mouth, this did not alleviate the obvious dryness that she was suffering. Finally, when I thought her relatively calm, although still clearly disoriented and out of time-synch, I ran upstairs, got some ice and raced back down. Although normally slow of foot, I was very fast this time.

"She chewed on some ice cubes and continued to get stuck on the 'not . . . not . . . not . . .' of the previous phrase describing the comet. Alan had returned home and at this juncture joined me in the bedroom. We stayed together for another half hour or so, during which time we got a small glass of milk into her stomach, gave her a calming massage, worked with her on the phrase 'not make believe' a number of times, and generally tried to calm the situation and get her to go to sleep.

"When Alan went upstairs, it was approximately 2:15 A.M."

When I woke up in the morning, I felt terrible, though considerably less disoriented than before. But all parts of my body ached, my stomach most of all. All day I kept murmuring, "I don't feel very good, Dickie." I also kept asking, "What happened to me last night?" I could recall only parts of it.

Dick suggested I had seen the comet again, but I knew that was not the case. "I didn't see the comet," I told him, "but I saw buildings toppling and people dying. It was horrible."

Beyond that, I had no idea who had taken me, how, or why. I really didn't want to know.

At noon Tauri appeared. As soon as she did, Dick reached for the tape recorder. He wanted me to hear the conversation later. But suddenly it occurred to him that there might be a way for me to hear the conversation as it was happening—not that anything of the sort had ever occurred before. Still, he asked Tauri if she could arrange that and to his surprise she said yes.

For me it was an extremely odd, though by no means unpleasant, situation. It is very difficult to put into words. I felt as if Tauri were standing off to my left side and I was hearing her speak from there. I could see my own body and when I looked at the eyes, I could see Tauri. If you have a hard time understanding that, I don't blame you. But that's as closely as I can describe the sensation. Later Dick asked me if I could see him. I told him I hadn't tried.

"We were aware of what went on last night," Tauri said. "While we didn't prevent it, we saw to it that there was no harm done to our channel. While there is a 'law and order' in the universe, there are those that work about the edges and in the cracks. What they do is not right, but it doesn't shade the law sufficiently to call them lawbreakers. You have the same kind of thing going on on Earth.

"It would not do any good or serve any purpose for me to tell you who they were or what they wanted. Suffice it to say they are trying their hardest to stop the echoes that go forth after my channel speaks—and echoes there are. No, they did not damage the channel internally, and we will try to alleviate the aches to the body when we finish our conversation."

Dick wanted to know which city the comet would strike, so that we could warn the people living there.

"Dick, do you think that those to whom you would speak would leave their homes and businesses and the rest of their materials on just the words of you and my channel? No, I don't either. They would want to know the exact time and date and month and then, even with that information, how many of them do you think would leave? Not very many, I'm afraid.

"The hardest thing, when you link into this kind of dialogue, coming from where it does, in another dimension—the hardest thing is to comprehend why the information stops when you think you need it most. Even harder to understand, perhaps, is that we would put into jeopardy your very free will if we were to tell you these things you ask about. It is important that you think and relate but not be given directives. You know that. It would be wrong any other way. *Directions, yes. Directives, no.* Happily, this is one channel who does not want to deal with specifics.

"No, it wouldn't do much good for my channel to know the location of what she saw. She cannot live with that futurism comfortably. And we certainly would never roll the screen to give specific dates and times. Best forget about trying to warn those directly in the line of one of the catastrophes before it happens."

Through the years Dick has agonized about not knowing the exact location the comet will strike. Today the space-born cataclysms I've seen or heard about from my extraterrestrial sources are being given strong media coverage.

Malcolm W. Browne noted in a New York *Times* story on December 23, 1986, "Some 83 baby planets large enough to cause more damage than a nuclear war regularly come close to the Earth. One missed the Earth in 1982 by only three million miles —a narrow squeak. Another asteroid came within a mere 650,000 miles of us in 1976."

Astronomers are acutely aware of the dangers. One of them is Clark R. Chapman of the Planetary Science Institute in Tucson. Chapman urges world leaders to prepare for the day when an asteroid or comet is discovered heading on a collision course with our planet. He and various colleagues have suggested that the path of such an object could be deflected by nuclear explosions.

Unfortunately, others have said, the precise path such an object might take is all but impossible to calculate, owing to numerous imponderables such as the effect gravitational forces from other astronomical bodies such as planets and the sun would have on the approaching comet or asteroid. The mathematical problems alone would take too long to resolve to help us; the Earth could be destroyed before all the calculating was done.

I regret to say that the means of deflecting the approaching comet as suggested by Clark Chapman and his colleagues will be tried and will fail. The nuclear device will not be accurate enough to re-route the comet from its deadly trajectory to planet Earth. Kari-on of Lathea made sure I observed this futile effort.

Browne writes, "Many cultures have spawned apocalyptic visions of a day of wrath when universal destruction will rain down from the skies. Some of these visions are in curious consonance with the hypothetical finales proposed by astrophysicists, who occasionally remind us that neither the Earth nor anything else will last forever."

These apocalyptic visions may not be products solely of the imaginations of these other cultures. They may come from memories of actual events, periods of devastating changes which reshaped the face of the earth and forced the human beings then living—the ones who survived—to adapt to a whole new world.

One of this century's most controversial theorists was the late Immanuel Velikovsky, a psychoanalyst whose wide-ranging interest in ancient history and modern science led him to write a series of books. Beginning with *Worlds in Collision* in 1950, he contended that cataclysmic events, such as close encounters with passing astronomical bodies, had occurred in historical time. He believed that such events played a major role in shaping the history of the human race.

Velikovsky's ideas have been mostly discredited today. Yet the idea that astrocataclysms have immeasurably affected the Earth is now widely discussed and much accepted. For example, some prominent scientists champion the idea that a giant comet's collision with the Earth had much to do with the extinction of the dinosaurs. Even those scientists who refuse to accept this as *the* explanation acknowledge that it could well have been one of a number of factors that precipitated that enigmatic period of prehistory in which the "great extinctions" occurred.

Life on Earth is an extremely delicate proposition. Rampaging comets and asteroids are not the only threats it faces from outer space. If, for example, our sun were suddenly to become less than three tenths of 1 percent brighter or dimmer, the Earth could turn into a baking, barren desert or a frozen arctic wasteland.

Unhappily, such an alteration in solar luminosity is more than a hypothetical possibility. In the past five years scientists have noted that available sunshine has been declining steadily at .019 percent a year. As of this writing that amounts to a loss of one tenth of 1 percent—which, if present trends continue, doesn't give us long to go before dire consequences are felt.

Scientists are saying we shouldn't worry, that this is probably the result of sunspot activity and, when that is over, the sun will return to normal. Other scientists aren't so sure. They point out that the luminosity decline caught everybody by surprise. It was not predictable and no one can honestly state for sure how this puzzling, and potentially alarming situation has come about.

Sunspot activity notwithstanding, planetary change is an ongoing process. Science is getting a picture of catastrophic events that have shaped our planet over its four-and-one-half-billion-year life. Geological time is recorded in thousands and billions of years. We tend to lose sight of the changes. "It takes millions of years to happen," people will say. Yes, that's true. Geological change occurs over far greater periods of time than man can comfortably view. When we speak of geological catastrophe at the S.T.A.R. House, with its breathtaking view of the Blue Ridge Mountains, we say, "Beautiful, isn't it? But I wouldn't have wanted to be here when it rose out of the ground over five-hundred million years ago!"

For any number of reasons, it is difficult to avoid the conclusion that some very great changes in the Earth and its inhabitants are not very far ahead of us.

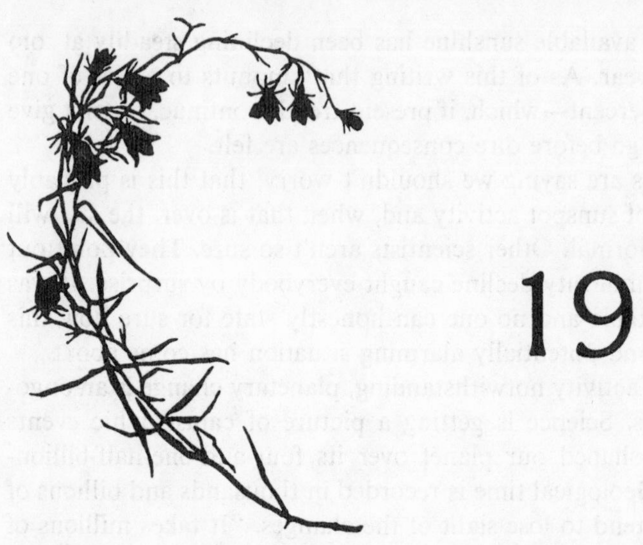

19

IN DECEMBER 1980 we traveled to San Diego to attend a meeting of the Young Presidents Organization, a group in which Dick and I had been very active members for many years. I had spoken to YPO groups in Little Rock and Dallas earlier that week, and now we had come to Southern California. We arrived on a Sunday evening, and I was scheduled to give a lecture in Newport Beach the following Tuesday. I was glad to have the day off to adjust to the different time zones before going up the coast.

Dick and I decided to take in a tour of Sea World. We joined a walking tour of the park and were enjoying the sights and sun when all of a sudden I became aware that someone was trying to enter the channel. I could sense that he was friendly, even though he seemed unfamiliar, and I also understood that he was going to share the channel with me. In other words, I would hear his words as he spoke them.

Later I learned that the entity's name was Aisill, from Oshan, and that he was a healer. Like many of his fellow Ogattans, he was scientifically inclined and enormously curious about the flora and fauna of our planet. This gorgeous park and aquarium held much that interested him.

The guide on our tour talked about the Torrey Pine, the tree indigenous to the Torrey Canyon where San Diego Sea World is located. (Hearing the name and not thinking of the spelling, I immediately thought of Tauri.) The guide pointed out the unusual features to the group and said that this particular species of evergreen lived only in that area. Aisill listened to those remarks and said, "We have trees in the jorpah but not on Tchauvi. But their main purpose is different. It is to provide a housing for the flowering plants that obtain their nourishment from the air. You also have air plants on your planet."

Of special interest to him, and to us, were the dolphins. Marine biologists have long recognized that dolphins possess unusual intelligence, though they are not sure if their intelligence is more or less than, or simply different from, ours. Some pioneering researchers, including John Lilly, have struggled to establish some means of communication with these remarkable creatures, with only limited success. Aisill, however, had no trouble.

Aisill appeared to know of human beings' great curiosity about dolphins and proceeded to enlighten us. Since the dolphin is a mammal, he compared it to the human species. Did we know that the brain capacity of the dolphin equals that of the human? Were we aware that it had evolved long before mankind and was in a fully developed state thirty million years before Man made his appearance on Earth? Did we know that before Man started polluting the oceans with motors that emit enormous noise the dolphins could communicate with any member of the species—any place in the world?

He tried to draw us out by asking Dick how many words the average human being has in his vocabulary. Dick guessed five thousand. Aisill replied that the average dolphin has ten thousand words in his vocabulary. He said dolphins "spoke syllabically" but offered no further explanation. A dolphin pup at eight to ten weeks of age has the emotional maturity of a human child eight to ten years old.

With that, Aisill made a fluttering motion with his (my) fingers and this brought three dolphins over to us. We assumed that there was more to this than the finger movement, though we heard no sound pass his lips. Telepathy seemed to be the real means of communication. For a period of time he stood with his attention focussed on the three motionless mammals, then walked away. Almost immediately the dolphins began making a clicking sound.

Aisill returned to the pool and again focussed his attention on the three creatures, all the while fluttering his fingers. After about sixty to ninety seconds he turned away. The dolphins no longer were "clicking."

"The dolphins were crying," Aisill explained to us. "I had to go back to conclude the communication so that they would not be unhappy. They so rarely come in contact with a 'human' with whom they can communicate that they did not want this meeting to end so rapidly."

We came to the killer whale exhibit. Aisill told us what we already knew, that "killer whale" is a misnomer, since these large sea mammals killed only to provide food and for no other reason. "They really are quite placid," he said. "The killer whale is a highly evolved animal, though not so evolved as the dolphin."

His knowledge of earthly aquatic animals proved remarkable. When we stopped at the predatory fish pool, he was able to point out the differences between the male and female members of a particular species of yellow-tailed fish. This was not something we would likely have been able to find out for ourselves, but when he pointed out these features, we could see, for instance, that the male had an aggressive expression on its face and the female a calmer, sweeter one. He told us the stingray has a facial expression on the underside of its body and if we could get one to roll over, we could actually see it "smile"! Obligingly, one flipped over in front of us after a flutter of Aisill's fingertips in its direction. It remained motionless for a minute or two and then Aisill waved it over and away.

A new penguin exhibit had just been opened and Sea World had reversed day and night so that marine biologists could study penguin living habits. They included two species of penguins of which the Emperor penguin was one.

Aisill pointed out the various penguin families. Again, these would not have been apparent to us, because there were large numbers of penguins standing together. But Aisill knew which belonged to which family. He was silent as our tour guide described the role the male Emperor penguin plays in hatching an egg. He takes it onto his feet, folds a flap of skin over it, and protects it for sixty-three days until it hatches. Aisill remarked that this "role reversal"—the male's taking an active role in the caring for the young—anticipated some of the role reversal that is now starting to take place in the human species. "There is much you can learn from birds and animals," he said.

(It is interesting to note that on a later occasion an entity would relate to us how Ogattans view sex roles. Dick and I were discussing women's fight for equality in the marketplace. A report had just come out stating that women performing the same jobs as men received only about 60 percent of the pay men did. The problem, we agreed, was the entrenched patriarchal nature of our society, which is just beginning to give way. As president of the Executive Search firm, I was keenly conscious of this aspect of economic inequality. An entity assumed the channel and entered the discussion. "In the jorpah," he said, "on all the five planets sex differences are largely social and ceremonial. Most times functions are undifferentiated by sex. It is the highest skills for the job that are sought. When a problem arises on any of the planets, the greatest talents and skills are brought in to solve the problem, regardless of which planet in the jorpah the most qualified reside on." What a quantum leap forward this practice would be on planet Earth!)

The next evening, as scheduled, I lectured to the group of young corporate presidents. They were all dynamic, golden men in the prime of life and business. After dinner one man approached me and asked if he could talk with me privately. I nodded and we walked into the lovely gardens surrounding the club. After some hemming and hawing he finally blurted out a very familiar "I have never told this to anyone before, *but—*" and proceeded to inform me that he could "never make a mistake in business." I smiled, remarking that since he was a highly successful businessman I didn't doubt that for a minute.

"No, no, you don't understand!" he exclaimed. "I *can not* make a mistake." And he fell silent. We kept walking and suddenly I had a psychic flash. "Do you communicate with crystal people?" I asked. The man's face crumbled and suddenly tears were rolling down his handsome cheeks.

"My God," he muttered. "Are there such things that others know about?" And he haltingly told me that whenever he has a major decision to make, a very tall being appears before him and in precise detail outlines what his course of action is to be. "He is never wrong," the man told me. "If I listen to his advice, my outcome is always profitable. He . . . he looks as if he were made of glass." He went on to repeat that he had never told a living soul, not even his wife, about this ongoing experience. "I'm not crazy, am I?" he asked me beseechingly.

I put my arms around him and assured him he was not. I offered to put him into contact with a politico who also talked with "crystal men," and he straightened up in excitement. He wanted to talk with that man *now.*

"Now?" I laughed. "Well, it's nine o'clock here in California but it's midnight in Washington. I'll connect you when I get back East."

"No, *now!*" he insisted.

And so the connection was made. I lost track of him over the years, but when last contacted, he told me he and the political figure had "set up a conference call for each Monday" to chat on the phone.

I will never understand why an entity from another (and presumably higher) dimension would be concerned in any way, shape, or form with an individual's business acquisitions or acumen. I have no answer to that question and it really doesn't matter. At the time I was baffled about how I came up with "crystal men"—clearly a purely psychic perception of what this man was unable to tell me in words. Since that time many persons have written to me about such beings.

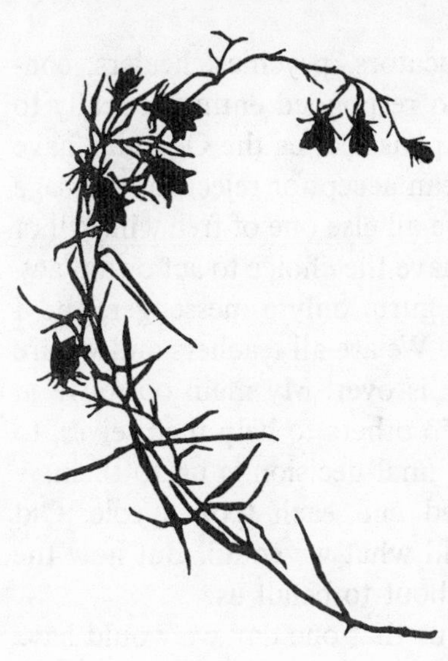

20

IN THE YEARS since the Ogattans have reentered my life, I've done all I can to spread the message. Dick and I have been around the nation and around the world and have met numerous people who in one way or another, directly or indirectly, are preparing themselves and others for the great changes to come. Some of our associations were short-lived. Others give every indication of being lifelong friendships.

I have spoken at business meetings, New Age gatherings, colleges and universities. I had a contract to speak for the American Stock Exchange. I have even been approached to be on many TV shows, including CBS's "60 Minutes," an invitation I turned down because I saw no way the full range of our experience and our message could be explained in a segment of thirteen minutes or less. Once I explained to the producer of "That's Incredible" that my life and my work were credible, not incredible, and no, I would not appear on his show. I realized too that, if the program's producers and reporters were so inclined, they could hold us up to public ridicule. I sent the same regrets to Geraldo for his show.

I have met world leaders, educators, psychics, healers, contactees, and ordinary citizens who responded enthusiastically to what I told them. All along I emphasized, as the Ogattans have repeatedly told us, that a person can accept or reject the message as one wished. The choice is above all else one of free will. All of us can believe or not believe and have the choice to act or not act. I tell my audiences that I am no guru, only a messenger, and I have no desire to be anything else. We are all teachers and we are all students. The day of the guru is over! My main objective in writing and speaking out is to help others to help themselves, to prepare for coming changes. The final decision is up to them.

Our children were all involved and each took a role. Old friends and new signed on. We did what we could. But now the biggest responsibility of all was about to befall us.

Quite early on, Tauri had told us that one day we would have to move. We heard this with decidedly mixed feelings. You don't lightly give up a life you have built and love: a home that has been the center of your world and a community of which you are very fond. You don't make an abrupt change of direction with blithe unconcern.

Tauri encouraged us to move. As always, she told us, "All we can do is suggest. The rest is up to you with your free will." But with that free will we had decided we were committed to the work. We would do what we had to do.

"Let me tell you something, dear Dick," Tauri said one day. "When you go to buy a book, you read for the most part, if you are like most human beings, from front to back. Maybe you read a couple of pages in the front, but you never read the ending first, do you? If you did, there would be no sense in buying the book. So I wrote the cover for you. And if you, through her, get a few glimpses of a couple of words just here and there, that's good, and you're supposed to. The final chapter is yet to be written by you and by her [Greta]. It is not there for you or for us to read. All we can do is suggest. The rest is up to you with your free will. *From the mountains that do not hold the snow, our channel will trumpet the voice, scribe the pen, and allay the fears.*

"I will lay it out for you both again.

"One: You should be where there is pure, fresh water. That is why we spoke of mountainous regions, but not so cold you need be concerned if you are without that to which you are accustomed, which is artificial heating.

"Two: Far enough away from the totally major industrial areas so that you need not be concerned [about] man's inhumanity to man.

"Three: Enough of a facility that those who come and who don't stay will have a place [which will] not intrude on your privacy, which you both hold dear and will hold even dearer.

"Four: Enough room to accommodate a family, perhaps larger than you think, from time to time.

"Five: A place where you can stockpile things you will need, whether it is for your frames or for others', external or internal.

"Six: Ground land to grow basics only, and not to be burdensome. Simply to help you over hurdles when the need arises. Fresh things to nourish human frames. And, yes indeed, things to gladden the eye and the other senses as well—the nose, the touch.

"Seven: Quartz in the mountains. Mountains which do not hold the snow.

"You wonder who will come, who will go, who will stay, who will not. That doesn't matter. What does matter is that the facility be there and the choice be yours and the invitation be yours. A place where people can come and go, but not stay. Refresh! Refurbish! Learn! You will absolutely be the captain of your own ship and guide your destiny to your Shangri La."

By that time, May 1980, we had made a trip into the Blue Ridge Mountains to investigate a possible site for our move, near Blowing Rock, North Carolina. It had most of the features we were looking for. We still had made no plans to sell our home in Westport and I was concerned about the strain of trying to run two large places at one time—places that, moreover, were far apart geographically. Dick and I had discussed these matters without resolving the issue. He was more for moving ahead and buying the second location before resolving the first than I was. On her next visit, we asked Tauri what she thought.

"I am not here to tell you whether it is or is not the right place," she said. "Let me say this to you. If indeed all of the guidelines that we would like for you to have cannot be found in the time frame that you set for yourself, then indeed you must compensate for that which you do not have. Know that we have no specific [place] in mind past the name of a girl, somewhere."

In her earliest communication on the subject, a year earlier, Tauri had told us there would be three or four false starts before we found what we were seeking. She also said it would be a "colossal deal," a "showpiece." This was a long way from what we had considered for our future when the children were grown: a turnkey existence in a condominium whose upkeep would not be a problem. What Tauri was outlining amounted to a major undertaking.

She told us to turn over the search for the property "to those who devote full time to finding such things as their livelihood" (real estate agents). In due course, thirty-six agents in the Carolinas, Virginia, and West Virginia (all girls' names) were out scouting for our property. They had our three pages of guidelines describing what we hoped to find. Some of the listings were non-tradable; others were hoped for but not essential. The pages described an overview of what we wanted to purchase: our dream for a New Age.

We went down into the Southern mountains several times, visiting places that were in one way or another unsatisfactory. It was a frustrating experience. Most of the time the problems with the locations were purely physical. On one occasion, though, the problem was psychic.

It was a property in North Carolina, really quite lovely, with five small buildings, two lakes, ample pastureland, and thirty acres. The agent was enthusiastic and Dick felt good on the land. I did not. I went and sat in the car. In fact, I wanted to get off the property as fast as possible. The agent was baffled by my behavior.

"Someone died violently here," I declared.

The agent was taken aback. "I don't think so," he said. "I've never heard anything like that." He turned to Dick, apparently expecting support.

But Dick was on my side. "If my wife says so," he remarked, "I would bet on it."

We didn't consider the property. But the agent, out of curiosity, investigated the history of the parcel. Sure enough, as he later told us, there had been a violent death there: a suicide.

In March 1982, even though we had yet to find our new home, we at last decided to sell our old one. It was a risky decision. Interest rates were sky high and people were not rushing out to buy new homes, and we were not exactly offering a low price. It could well be a long time before we found a buyer.

Nonetheless, before announcing the house's availability, we dutifully drew up a pictorial brochure and took it to the printers. As the brochure was being printed, a man walked in and bought the house for cash! We were, needless to say, not prepared for this, and it brought me a fresh set of worries such as: Where were we going to stay until we found our place in the mountains?

Fortunately the buyer let us rent what had been our house until the end of the year. That eased the immediate problem but I still felt pretty uneasy. Every person has a sticking point. My home is basic to my feelings of security and I was, essentially, without a home. Dick kept trying to reassure me.

"We've got the money in the bank from the sale of the house," he would say. "We can buy whatever and whenever we want. It's just a matter of finding it." Those eminently reasonable words didn't help me much. I was as nervous as a cat.

Meanwhile I continued my lectures. Dick and I would write them together—he did most of the texts—and I would put them into my own words. A year before, I had published a book, *On a Slide of Light,* which had attracted attention and was bringing in daily mail and requests for appearances. In addition, we had started a bimonthly newsletter, *The Woodrew Update,* which had a growing circulation. Those who read the book wanted to stay in touch, and our newsletter provided the perfect vehicle. As suggested by the Ogattans, I was trumpeting the voice and scribing the pen. To all appearances readers and audience members were receiving the message enthusiastically. Still, with all the uncertainties at that moment in our lives, I was battling insecurities.

As usual Dick did what he could to help. He asked Tauri, "Did you notice the impact the channel had on all those people when we were in Hawaii?"

"I know," Tauri replied. "The important thing is: Did you notice? I have been telling you all along—she will again sway crowds with that voice of hers."

I appreciated that vote of confidence, but I continued to feel that without a home to call my own, my effectiveness as a communicator was going to be compromised. It was illogical but so was I. The search went on.

In July 1982 we found exactly what we were looking for, a property a dozen miles outside Waynesville, North Carolina. We were enthralled. The ground seemed to be charged with an energy which we could both sense. There was another place, too, not far away, which gave us much the same feeling, but it was not as accessible (with easy directions) for those who would come and go in the future.

We put in a bid on the first place. Our offer turned out to be a great deal less than the owner wanted. The discussion with the realtor and owner ended with no further dialogue. We were sorely disappointed but had no choice other than to go on with the search—an indefinite search, it now appeared.

Over Labor Day we visited our good friends, octogenarians Harold and Martha Sherman, in Arkansas. If you have never heard of him, you should know that Harold is a truly remarkable man: one of our greatest living psychics and author of over a hundred books which make sense of ESP and its "how-to's" in a way few others do.

Harold's most celebrated psychic feats took place during what British television producer Adam Hart-Davis has called "the greatest experiment in mental telepathy of the century." During the winter of 1937–38 Harold, who then lived in New York City, acted as "receiver" of thoughts sent by Arctic explorer Sir Hubert Wilkins thousands of miles away. The experiment, which occurred over a two-and-a-half-month period, was so successful that Reginald Iversen, the man assigned by the New York *Times* to maintain radio contact with the explorer, stated, "Sherman actually had a more accurate knowledge of what was happening to Wilkins . . . than I was able to gain in my ineffective attempts to keep in touch by shortwave radio." Sherman and Wilkins later wrote a famous book about their experiment, *Thoughts Through Space* (1942).

In the course of our friendship with him, we have seen repeated examples of Harold's astonishing psychic perception. I asked if he would try to "see" when we would find our place.

He closed his eyes, rested his hands on the kitchen table and remained totally still for about three minutes. Then, opening his eyes, he looked at us and said, "On October tenth you will buy your property."

We asked him to describe the house. He responded with a perfect description of the Waynesville property for which we had bid and been rejected. We had been told there was no hope of further negotiation.

We said nothing of this to Harold, but later, as Dick and I discussed the matter, we concluded that Harold's psi had taken him backward, rather than forward, in time.

On October fifth we received a call from a broker, reopening the Waynesville possibility. We flew to North Carolina on the seventh and revised our offer.

On the tenth Dick, not even remembering the date Harold Sherman had foreseen, told me, "Today I am going to buy our house." He called the owner and told him that he would buy a house today. He hoped it was his. But if the offer was not acceptable, he would buy another we had seen. We upped the bid somewhat and the offer was accepted.

Hours later, as we were in the car headed for the airport, Tauri assumed the channel. We pulled over to the side of the road.

"So you found Reisha Way, did you?" she asked. "Are you happy now?" "Reisha," she informed us, is an Ogattan word for "high healing energy." And so now not only did we have our home, we had a name for it: Reisha (REE-sha) Way.

"Gee," I said to Dick. "It sounds like a geisha house. But I guess Tauri named it for us. So Reisha Way it shall be."

"Sometimes you don't listen to all of the clues," she rebuked us good-humoredly. We thought we had worked them to death! (Later we realized that the clue about a "girl's name" had to do, probably, with "Carolina" but, more specifically, with the nearby town of Maggie Valley—and, even more specifically, with our own interstate exit, *Maggie.)* We told her we felt we had needed more direction but we knew better than to ask for it.

Her reply staggered us. She said, "We telepathized not only the date but the description of the house for you when you were in Arkansas with a master of telepathy. Thoughts can be sent from any place in the cosmos, you know."

We know now. We called Harold to confirm the accuracy of his prediction, to thank him, and to rejoice.

Reisha Way was ours. Our future direction had found its base. We could begin the new life.

21

I AGONIZED over what direction the small part we would play would take when the Earth changes began to step up more visibly. In preparation, I started to deliver lectures all over the world. Dick and I put our combined efforts into *The Woodrew Update,* the international newsletter begun in 1981. I was "trumpeting the voice and scribing the pen," but surely there was more to it than that?

Great time was consumed in personally answering the flood of (now) more than eleven thousand letters that came in response to my first book, the lectures, and the *Update.* An unavoidable hour or two a day was spent on the phone with callers seeking answers to their own extrasensory experiences. "I don't feel so alone any more. Thank you for sharing . . ."

It was a major transition to move from a home in which we had lived and loved for twenty-nine years. It was like a rebirth to begin again with the rebuilding necessary to our new location. I recall the trauma attached to seeing our whole married life packed into a huge moving van. "Almost thirty years, and it's all in *there?*" Dick murmured.

In addition to the overwhelming physical demands associated with our new life, there were changes in myself with which to cope as well. I sat down and wrote what, in essence, was a letter to myself. It was printed in our newsletter:

> I am learning the art of accepting myself for what I am. More than that, I recognize the need to change my view of myself—and of change itself. There are no trains to yesterday, so today's ride has to be on board a new train of thought and behavior if I am to cope with tomorrow.
>
> The difficult part is taking responsibility for my changes without blocking any progress. The truth of the matter is—I am impatient. My life-style is enhanced when I can "plan my work and work my plan" efficiently.
>
> In these uncertain days of my relocation this is not always possible. It's not the thirteen rooms filled with accumulated treasures (junk?) that boggle my mind. It's the numerous bundles of memories stacked into every corner and which have been expanding for three decades. Can I move them without damage? What insurance covers their move?
>
> I can take the overstuffed albums of pictures of my children, friends, gardens, but . . . they are only reproductions. It is stressful to contemplate. Change is stressful. Humans do not react well to change.
>
> So I am learning a great deal about this human "creature of habit" who lives inside this "creature of action" . . . and taunts me with "what if's"—but never with doubts.

There were hilarious moments. There was, for example, the letter we received from Jill. All of our children were delighted with what was happening but a bit baffled at trying to describe our work to the uninitiated. Jill wrote:

> Here's a typical conversation with my colleagues at *Newsweek.*
>
> "So what's new?"
>
> "My folks recently moved to North Carolina."
>
> "Oh, did they retire?"
>
> "No, they decided they needed a change of scenery."
>
> "What are they going to do down there?"
>
> "They're involved in some research of their own."

"What kind of research?"

Now here is the problem. I can't just blurt out, "Oh, they deal with matters outside the current paradigms." Or, "They're conducting psychic experiments." And I can't launch into a three-hour discourse on the Ogatta Group. So I say something precise, like, "Gee, I think I hear my phone ringing and I'm expecting a call from our correspondent in Nicaragua." I hope Tauri and the other friends don't feel slighted, but what's the daughter/reporter of a psychic to do?

Ordered chaos reigned. We were getting into the Waynesville swing of things. We oversaw the work of carpenters, electricians, and plumbers—all honest, decent folk who became friends. Some, unfortunately, had a disregard for time.

If some tradespeople say they will be there tomorrow at 9:00 A.M., you can probably—make that possibly—depend on them for three days from tomorrow. Or next week. All the while they have the best of intentions, and absolutely no sense that they have inconvenienced you. It's not that they're forgetful. They'll tell you that the tobacco needed hoeing or a friend asked them to help move some logs, or they had to get in a bit of firewood before they came. In deer-hunting season they "get gone." Telephone to let us know? "Well, I guess I should have . . ." Mostly, though, they're surprised that you don't understand.

These wonderful people have lived for many, many years close to the soil, close to the seasonal rhythms of spring and fall and summer and winter. Their lives are marked by these long, slow rhythms.

Change is often unpredictable. But it is predictable that when change hits, human beings will do all in their power to impose comfortable old habits on new situations.

We were no exception. We promptly slipped into an old habit that we both find reassuring: drawing up schedules and then getting things done "on time." We were determined to continue this custom even if it conflicted with some customs of new neighbors.

It was a challenge, but slowly and surely, just as it had been with our friends and dinner guests in Westport, the mountain people learned that when we said 9:00 A.M. tomorrow, we meant

9:00 A.M. tomorrow. Beyond this, we had no desire to impose our ways on them. At the same time we were not about to allow them to impose their ways on us.

In due course we carefully put together a cooperative group of skilled craftsmen: carpenters, plumbers, electricians, bulldozer men, painters, carpet layers, stone-masons. They would eventually be called on to work on the big project, the S.T.A.R. House. We number this crew among our new friends.

The first six to eight months were devoted to adapting the rooms in our new house to our tastes. Utility and comfort are subjective qualities and all owners must put their individual stamp on a house before it fully becomes their home.

We arranged open spaces within the house to handle our needs and those of visitors comfortably. We built offices and a library to accommodate our work habits, and installed sliding glass doors to improve our view of the Blue Ridge and Smokies, two great mountain ranges that, when you look out the west windows, meet.

Those two mountain ranges are reputed to be the oldest in America. A former governor of the state, Jim Hunt, claimed that they were the oldest mountains in the world, being Precambrian, or over six hundred million years old. The variety and number of species of flora exceed those of any other range in the world, making the scenery truly wondrous.

Slowly we got the attributes of the gracious life-style we cherish out of their packing cases: our crystal, linens, silver, the paintings and sculptures, the bone china; the lovely things that over the years had become part and parcel of our way of life. They remain part of our daily living and will continue to do so for as long as this civilization allows: perhaps only a few short years, but years to be treasured. Yes, let there be candlelight, embroidered tablecloths, and shining sterling for as long as possible. We have earned the right to enjoy them. But when it can no longer be, we have made plans for an immediate survival posture, stark and essential; "no frills," as the saying goes.

Only after we had satisfied ourselves with the inside did we tackle the landscape outdoors. We planted over eight thousand rhododendron, mountain laurel, locothia, azalea. Two Connecticut friends came to help, and the land began to take on the look of our living. We brought part of the outdoors inside by building a greenhouse addition to our bedroom.

Always our friends, members of our "extended family," came. They knew the work we were doing and wanted to be part of it. Experts in many fields found their way to Reisha Way from all over the world. We would meet them at the Asheville airport, and rejoice in their elation at the scenery during the thirty-five-mile drive home. They would respond to the unique beauty of Reisha Way and contribute their own abilities and talents to our projects.

Meanwhile, I was being invited to lecture all over the world, and we took the time to trumpet the voice. I lectured in South Africa, Switzerland, Holland, Bermuda, and all over Canada and the United States. It took time and effort to be away from Reisha Way, but it was intensely rewarding. And from every audience, from every nation, we would bring back new information: "think and relate" material. There was one phrase we heard repeatedly: "It's never been as . . ." We could fill in the rest: hot, cold, dry, wet. The changes are coming, fast.

By the end of 1984 we were ready to start on a separate facility for S.T.A.R. Foundation's work. Originally, we intended to build the S.T.A.R. House by radically remodeling our five thousand-square-foot barn, which had a colossal mountain view as backdrop.

Bob Andron, a solar expert, New Age architect, and good friend living in Raleigh, North Carolina, had volunteered to draw up plans for the facility. But we had no idea what projects the S.T.A.R. House would serve. We had been told that we would need it, that the people who would use it would come. But what people and for what purpose? Bob, Dick, and I agonized over the plans for months.

We used the word "facility" because of its dual meaning of both "structure" and "freedom from difficulty." We envisioned a facility that would make any project flow smoothly and effortlessly. Certainly the setting itself would foster a congenial and harmonious work environment.

We had two absolutes: water independence and energy independence. The key word for the interior was to be "flexibility."

We expected to accommodate groups of up to seventy-five or eighty for activities ranging from lectures, colloquiums, and seminars to research and healing sessions. The space, we decided, should allow for gracious if light eating, occasional sleeping for ten, study and discussion, a media center and food, medical supply, clothing, and furniture storage. Under extreme conditions it should be able to house those passing through in transition. We emphatically were not planning to run a hotel.

Eventually we decided that the beautiful barn was not satisfactory for the purposes we had in mind but should remain as it was: a barn. In emergencies it could house dozens of people. With that in mind, we stocked in sixty sleeping bags. So we started from scratch, with plans that we found out later made for extremely complicated building.

Dick (who had never built so much as a doghouse) was the general contractor on the job, and the crews we had gathered over the months were the "subs." Dick studied intensely, as he does any subject he undertakes. He laid out the area in slanted sections to maximize the passive solar aspect. This gave each part of S.T.A.R. House its own particular and spectacular view of the mountains.

All the men worked with enthusiasm. They had a mental picture of what we were building; what it needed to become and what we hoped for. Miracle of miracles, it came out even better than we had visualized. As I told Dick, "Darling, you went from being the best G.C. on Rabbit Skin Road to the best G.C. in the county to the best G.C. in the world!" He'd grin and say, "Well, I upgraded the materials and still brought it in under cost. What a blast!"

S.T.A.R. House is built partially underground, bermed into the side of our mountain. This feature provides the strength and the climatization of an "earth house." We used redwood siding outside and tongue-in-groove ash on interior walls. Tremendous quantities of Cherokee stone on many other walls emit feelings of great strength and power. According to our friend Dr. Philip Callahan, the energies of this stone "actually infuse into your body from the crystalline rocks." These rocks act as solar collectors as well, adding a high energy quotient. Ancients were experts at working with the magnetic emissions from stone as well as the light from the sun.

We trapped a spring to supply the water to S.T.A.R. House by force of gravity—gravity-feed—a delicate task of exposing the spring without diverting or burying it. The soil-conservation people master-minded the project. It was the first time we had ever availed ourselves of government expertise. They were terrific!

We have learned how to handle the "traffic flow" of our many visitors and guests. We installed video equipment, a raised podium incorporating the latest electronics and plenty of room for an audience. Numerous healings have taken place at the house and we have held several major conferences for our Updaters, S.T.A.R. supporters, CEOs, and members of the Young President's Organization (YPO). As befits our purpose, our logo, the Greek "psi" symbol, is worked into and onto our Cherokee stone walls. The sign of that fateful comet is depicted in iron railings and furniture fabrics.

What the house's long-range uses will be, we still do not know with certainty, but Tauri assures us that it will serve the purpose for which it will be needed. For now, all we know is that our personal scenario is on schedule: in place by 1984. A building year, 1985. A storage year, 1986. A writing year, 1987. Another book in 1988. We have "trumpeted the voice and scribed the pen." And, we hope, we have been "allaying the fears." We are not apologetic about what we are doing; not to dear friends who do not and cannot understand, not to strangers who decide we are either kooks or elitists, not to those who feel we have thrown away what would be extraordinarily useful lives in what they call "the real world." Not to anyone.

The Ogattans visit us here, to delight us, to refresh us, to encourage us. Now that we have made our decisions and our move, now that we are entering with zest on our new life, they call on us less often for purely playful reasons. They reiterate that all is "right on target." We treasure the memories of their comic/cosmic playfulness in our indoctrination period. They still play games but much less often than they used to.

There was the time, for example, when they moved all of our furniture around and waited in anticipation for our expressions of astonishment. Once they had heard those, they moved it all back! Another time they moved a Steinway grand piano from one room to another, although it could not possibly have been moved through the archway between the two rooms. Later, they returned it to the living room from the dining room—in about as much time as it takes to blink an eye.

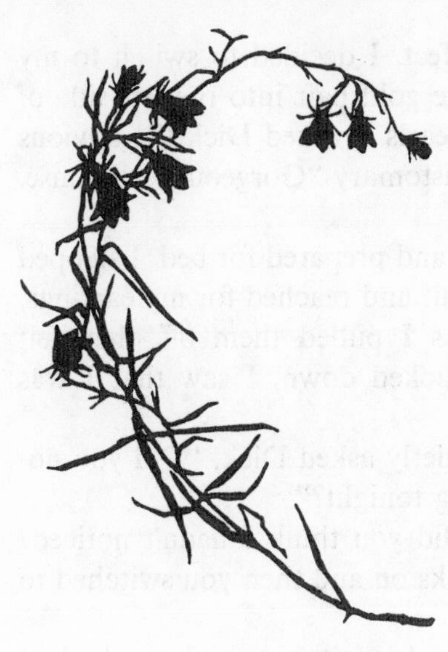

22

THEN THERE was the episode of the earrings.

Two years ago our daughter Jill got married in New York. We stayed with close friends in their apartment in the city for the weekend of festivities.

During that hectic period I wore and lost a carved ivory earring. The pair had been a favorite of mine since 1978, when Dick had bought them for me on our trip to China. Though not especially valuable, I wore them all the time and with great pleasure.

I begged our host and hostess to comb the apartment for the earring. They did, but to no avail. I kept the remaining one in a drawer of my telephone table, unwilling to throw it away. "Some day," I told Dick, "friends will go to Canton and maybe they can find a matching earring for me."

I have two other pair of favorites: my father-in-law's cuff links (made over into handsome gold earrings) and my grandmother's pearls. Unlike the ivory, they are both beautiful and valuable.

Recently we had occasion to attend a gathering for which it was necessary to dress up. I went into my closet, automatically reached for the cuff link earrings, fastened them on, stepped over to the mirror and studied the effect. I decided to switch to my grandmother's set, and tossed the gold pair into the left side of the drawer as I clipped on the pearls. I asked Dick the obvious "How do I look?" and got the customary "Gorgeous!" response, and we left the house.

Hours later we returned home and prepared for bed. I stepped over to the closet, hung up my suit and reached for my earrings, intending to put them away. As I pulled them off, they felt strange in my hands. When I looked down, I saw that I was holding the ivory earrings.

Closing my hands tightly, I quietly asked Dick, "Did you notice which earrings I was wearing tonight?"

He laughed and answered, "Did you think I hadn't noticed? First you had my father's cuff links on and then you switched to your grandmother's pearls."

When I didn't respond, he walked over to me, took one look at my face and spoke gently. "What's wrong? Did you lose one?"

I unclenched my hands and let him see the ivory earrings, one in each palm. "The Ogattans," he said.

"How else?" I whispered, tears rolling down my cheeks.

He went to the telephone table and opened the drawer in which the single had lain since the loss of its mate. There was nothing there. I opened the locked drawer in my closet where jewelry is kept and the two gold earrings I had tossed to one side were lying neatly side by side with the pearl set, dead center in the drawer.

The Ogatta group also took note of another important date in our lives: Dick's birthday in the summer of 1986. That one turned out to be a birthday to end all birthdays.

It had been a lovely day all along, with calls, cards, and assorted gifts. The children had given Dick a wall unit depicting an Alaskan scene over which he had flipped the previous winter. I presented him with a piglet named "E.I." (as in "E-I-E-I-O") to join the menagerie of Dick's special animal friends. Later a group of friends arrived with a home-baked, decorated cake and books. Then all of us went to a dinner theater.

When that was all done, Tauri showed up. For twenty minutes

she talked with Dick about "galaxies in the near universe." Finally she said she, too, had a gift. She brought in a gattae, close enough so that its whirling colors could be observed but not near enough to see beyond the elliptical shape of the spaceship.

Dick's myopia prevented him from seeing much, but Tauri took care of that. She passed a hand in front of his eyes and his vision expanded immediately and miraculously. Now he could see the red, yellow, green, and blue lights distinctly.

The craft hovered about eight hundred feet away, atop the peak facing our terrace from the southwest. Dick and I sat in stunned delight and watched the lights pulse. To our unspoken request Tauri said, "We cannot bring it in any closer. This is not the time to take you inside."

We nodded, swept up in the beauty and excitement of the moment.

It was a very cloudy night, allowing no starlight to peek through, so with another pass of the hand she moved the clouds to reveal a star-studded sky. We turned to exclaim over the brightness of the almost-full moon, a lopsided beauty hanging in the sky where she had "opened it up" for us. When we turned back to the south side to see the gattae—it was gone. It had vanished in a blink, with no sound whatsoever.

We sighed deeply and Tauri chuckled. "Another time, another night," she promised us.

Tauri stayed on to confirm that the Scenario of change is still "on target" and to encourage us with our preparations. She talked about the other channels, elsewhere in the world, also being readied to assist the Ogatta group "in our time of transition." She answered a question about our China experience. Incredibly, it turned out that we had indeed spent an afternoon with "a channel in training" in Shanghai, China, in 1978. (The man did not know of his cosmic connection then. He does now.) I recalled the incident, a most unusual one.

The group we were with in China was among the first to be gathered from business leaders in the United States, following the opening of relations between the two nations. What made this group unique was that each of the men was chief executive officer of his company, and 90 percent of the group were doing business with China through a foreign subsidiary or company. Therefore, at each stop we made, some local company official or representative of local industry appeared to meet with one or more of our companions. The effect of all this was to make us feel closer to China and its wonderful people.

In Shanghai the local leaders arranged for us to make a trip around the city's harbor with students from a local college. They were learning English for future use as travel guides, translators, or diplomats. The channel in training was one of these delightful Chinese students.

We were both on the boat going for a tour around the harbor. When we looked at each other, both of us suddenly, inexplicably knew the other. Each of us exclaimed, "I know you!" He had never been outside Shanghai and I had never been to the Chinese mainland. "But I know you!" we kept repeating in utter bewilderment.

"In another lifetime?" I suggested. But he shook his head and said, "No, no. I know you."

The strangest part of this meeting became apparent when we returned to the United States and had our film developed. A picture of the two of us—round, green-eyed American and tilted brown-eyed Chinese—revealed that, when you blocked out all facial features except the area of the eyes, you could not distinguish which were mine and which were his. It was very strange.

We mentioned this to Tauri and she was casual about it.

"If you put all of the Ogattan channels' eyes together," she said, "you would find yourself unable to differentiate among them. The eyes are the doorways of the soul."

There was an amusing aftermath to this meeting. Wanting to do something especially nice for me, the Chinese student handed Dick a tiny pin he was wearing on his lapel. "For you. Because . . . your wife . . . I *know* her," he stammered. Dick thanked him and I blew him a kiss from the bus when we were ready to leave Shanghai. Dick wore the pin everywhere.

Our next stop was Canton and the Canton Business Fair. As Dick is wont to do, he wandered off down a strange street to get the feeling of the city. Suddenly I heard a commotion. As I looked to find the cause, along came Dick walking literally head and shoulders above close to a hundred Chinese men and women. They were following him in considerable humor, laughing behind their hands and pointing to his pin. When Dick loudly proclaimed, *"Shanghai!"*, the crowd would all go "Ahhhhh!" Then the process would be repeated a few feet further along.

Our friends and I, watching him approach, were hysterical. We finally found a Cantonese translator who told us the reason the crowd was following Dick. The little pin was from the Young Communist Party! It wasn't the Communist part that fascinated and amused the Chinese; it was the "Young." All YCP members were under thirty. It was obvious that Dick didn't meet the age requirement.

Needless to say, we put the pin away. But we kept it as a memento of a wonderful young man—a channel—who "knew" me as I "knew" him. "Oh, but Tauri, a *Communist* channel?!" I exclaimed. Her tinkling laughter is still with me: "My dear channel, from where we sit, we just view you as humans."

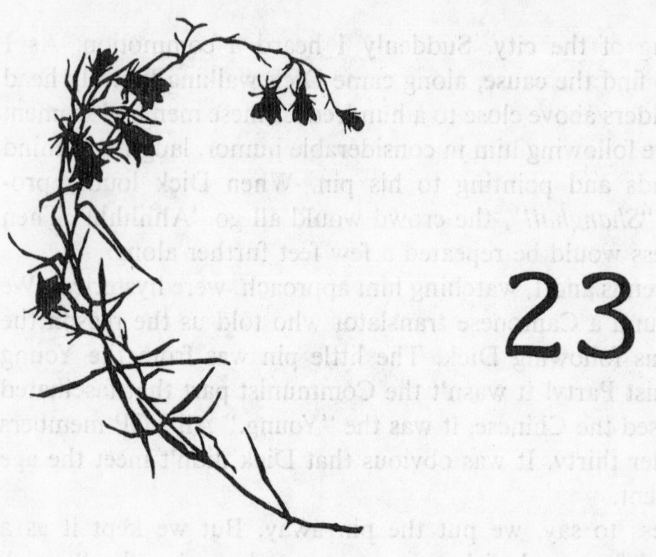

23

FOR MANY YEARS I had been a healer of others. I had no occasion, nor had it occurred to me, to heal myself. Until, that is, one day at the very end of 1985.

It was snowing and I was on an errand for a neighbor, to pick up some Christmas candles ten miles down the road. I got into my Jeep station wagon and, driving at a cautious ten miles per hour, I started wending my way down the mountain.

Then, in an instant, the car was lurching wildly out of control. I had hit a patch of concealed ice. Steering in the direction of the spin, I saw that I was headed for an eight-foot-drop embankment. Directly under it stood a trailer and a car. My only thought was, "Dear God, don't let me kill anyone!" Then everything went into slow motion.

Out of control, the Jeep hit the shoulder on the side of the road and turned crazily upside down. I could see the trailer looming up below me. I heard glass shatter and steel crunch as the car turned over again and I plummeted over the side of the embankment. I threw myself on my side, covering my face before the final impact.

All of this could have taken no more than four seconds, but it seemed an eternity.

The next thing I knew, an old man limped out of another trailer and very haltingly asked, "Are you alive?"

"I think so," I said.

At that moment being alive felt like a mixed blessing. Pain was shooting through my neck, legs, and knees, and my hair and coat were covered with shattered glass from the windshield and windows. I realized I had slivers of glass all over my face and hands. And then I realized they were also in my eyes.

The front doors of the car were crushed shut, so I slowly crawled over the front seat and climbed out of the back door. The old man led me to his trailer to call for help after I told him I did not want an ambulance. I called my house and asked Charles, who then worked for us, to come and get me. "I have car problems," I said.

Charles found me standing in the road, glittering with glass but steady. The car, at rest eight feet below the road, was utterly demolished.

"Let's go!" I said. "Take me to the opthomologist's office."

When we got to a bend where we should have turned left, I asked him to go right. "Might as well pick up those candles," I said, not terribly rationally. (Later Charles told me he was not about to argue with someone in obvious shock.) We went five miles (each way) out of our way to get the candles.

I asked Charles not to talk to me. "Just get me to the eye specialist," I said. I closed my eyes and focussed on them.

When we arrived, the opthomologist removed two pieces of glass from my eyes as well as numerous slivers. He detected four or five abrasions on my corneas. He said I would be all right in a couple of weeks and I ought not to worry about my vision or the pain because tiny glands would swell under the lids after all his probings. "You'll have a sensation of glass still being in there," he warned me, "but keep your eyes closed as much as possible for the rest of the day. Now, you ought to go to the hospital and be checked out." He spoke in a tone of gentleness and concern.

My thoughts were moving in slow motion: "I'm cold, in

shock." "What will they do to me at the hospital? X-ray? Fluoroscope? Give me a sedation? No. I don't want any of that." I am ever reluctant to allocate responsibility to others for my wellness.

I got back into the car with Charles and said, "Drive me home, please. Forgive me, but I do not want to talk."

During the twenty-minute drive I kept my eyes closed, my hands running up and down over my increasingly aching knees and whiplashed neck. I needed the kind of miracle I had worked for others.

As soon as we got home, I issued brief instructions: "Please bring me heating pads and cold compresses, and then I wish to be left entirely alone for six hours. No calls, no food. And above all else, no chatter." I certainly didn't want to talk about how that old man had told me that exactly a year ago, in the same spot, a man careened off that embankment and went into the trailer, killing his daughter-in-law, who was pregnant with twins.

The time stayed in slow motion. I knew that icebags were called for (on my swelling knees, banged-up legs, and abdomen) but I somehow sensed that swelling later was preferable to using ice at the moment. I needed heat. I piled another quilt onto my bed, put the heating pads on my knees, the cold compresses on my eyes. Then I lay on my back and became very, very still.

"Talk to your body," I commanded myself. "You'll make it."

I ached for Dick. But he was driving to Florida and I was scheduled to fly there to meet him the next day for my brother's wedding. I had a running monologue inside my head:

"I am in shock. Nothing feels broken. If there are any internal injuries, I can set them aright. My eyes. I must take care of my eyes first. Then the whiplash to my neck which is suddenly so painful. And my knees. Well, I'll just work 'down' the body. I can do it."

These things played over and over in my head as I lay there for that six-hour stretch. I applied total concentration to my body and my becoming well. I zeroed in to bringing about a well condition to my whole being, knowing that the healing phenomenon bears out Plato's dictum that healing begins with the mind and the soul.

We have a greenhouse addition in our bedroom, where plants bloom all year round. They all lean toward the sun and glass and away from the direction of the bed. But when I opened my eyes, after the six hours, every blossom in the room was turned toward the bed, literally leaning in toward me. I had held myself in close check but now I cried. I felt as if, at some level of sentience, these plants were giving me back some of the love I had lavished on them. And then, when I looked into the mirror, I saw that my eyes looked fine. They were not red or bloodshot, as I had every expectation they would be. My body, though black and blue, was not swollen.

The next day, after a night of attempting cell-to-cell communication within my body, I went to the airport, got to my brother's wedding the next day, and danced—shakily, perhaps, but it was dancing.

I was determined not to talk about the accident or what might have been, even with my children. Of course I talked with Dick, asking him this question that had been haunting me: How did the car land sideways, eight inches from the trailer on the right and six inches from a car on the left? A professional driver couldn't have edged it into that space at that angle with a car which had flipped over an embankment, out of control.

A week later Tauri told Dick, our son Alan, and me that I had indeed healed myself, "putting together many lessons given in the cosmos," and that while the accident was entirely an earthly affair, the landing "might have had a bit of help from higher energies other than themselves."

For months afterward the slow-motion crash played and replayed before my eyes. "Why am I alive?" I kept asking myself. I was, needless to say, grateful to have been spared, but I wondered how it had happened. All I knew was that I remained to do the work I was to do.

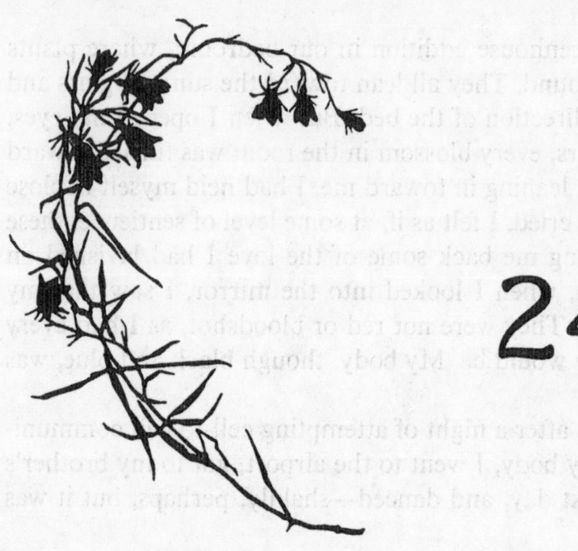

24

LIVING IN THE MOUNTAINS has been like reentering the classroom. There are so many skills to learn, so many activities to observe, so many things to do.

For me it is an aerobic walk in the mountains every morning, before I start work. It would be so easy to be in the mountains and yet never get to know them with my feet, my breathing (that glorious, clear air!), to feel their energies, to partake of their beauty, to be part of their vibrations.

Dick is up at 6:30 A.M. daily, to accomplish what he calls his "chores." These involve seeing our four-legged friends. There are the house-friends: three dogs (Ufo, Crystal, and Spock) and four cats (Yoda, Pi, Cosmo, and Tom). The dogs always eagerly await his coming so that they can accompany him to visit the goat-pen dwellers: two billy goats, Banjo and Fillet, both born on our land. Then there is Lambchop, a beautiful black-faced sheep, and there are Hada (as in "Mary Hada Little Lamb") and our two new ewes, Streisand (after Baa-bra) and Cybill (Sheepherd). Rambo I, our white-faced ram, is the macho member of the herd, who demands attention. Another member of the clan is our beautiful llama, Dalai. (Everyone should have a Dalai llama, my anniversary gift to Dick and surely the most photographed llama on this planet—second only, that is, to Karma the llama, with his incredible long eyelashes, my subsequent birthday present to Dick.) And E.I., our fast-growing pig.

The goat-pen dwellers live in total harmony but differ aggressively in their eating habits. Because of this Dick uses a separate technique to feed Karma, who would otherwise lose his food to the goats. He puts a leash on Karma's muzzle and walks him like a big dog, grooming him as they go, and feeding him out of his "magic pocket," which contains a mixture of horse and rabbit pellets and alfalfa hay. Karma is very gentle and children love to pet him.

Lambchop formed the habit of following to the gate where Dick leashed Karma, so one day he let her come along. After that she became a regular member of the parade. Then Hada joined the walk, and sometimes Rambo. The Dalai llama impatiently waits for their safe return "home," after the gang collects eggs from our "Chicken Hilton" and gives a carrot or sugar cubes to Star and Patsy, our patient and not-very-bright riding horses.

Anyone driving into Reisha Way around seven-thirty in the morning is apt to see a weird person, jeans-clad, walking his pet llama and sheep, alfalfa hay dripping from his pockets, with dogs and cats rubbing against his legs as he walks, or running off to explore the woods. Mother blue jays leave their nests and babies to greet the processional. Rabbits stop their hopping and stare. Even the chickens let Dick pet them, although Doodle-do, the rooster, ignores him.

Thus the parade reaches the barn and pasture. During the summer we have plenty of good grazing pastureland. During the winter months, even in this land where "the snow does not stay," our horses and llamas need supplementary hay and feed grain.

Ours is a mountain of tranquility, where cooperation replaces territoriality. It works in the microcosm. The Ogatta group tells us it also works in the macrocosm. In fact, the Ogatta group stresses the need for man's cooperation with all species, both flora and fauna, to insure our survival in the changing times ahead. Lest we forget, the Ogattans remind us that we are the only species on the planet incapable of communicating totally within our own species.

This is the life of the mountains, even with all else we have to do. Even with the work at our desk, the eleven thousand letters we have received (each with its own thoughts and suggestions, each with its personalized character), and that I have personally answered. Even with our newsletter, the *Update,* to prepare, the lectures to get ready, the radio programs to work on, this book to write. Even with the studying that must be done, the many and varied magazines and newspapers that must be scanned, the tapes that must be made ready. Even with the daily visitors, phone calls, healings.

The beauty of our planet has become so much more focussed for us here. The sunsets seem brighter, the twilights duskier, the stars closer. We each feel fifteen years younger than when we arrived. In my eyes, Dick looks much younger than he did in his suit-and-tie commuting days.

But even here we can see the changes coming. The warm seasons are shorter, the cold ones longer. The newspapers we read and the television news we watch tell us of the increasingly erratic behavior of people. The world climate is producing records. Our local area experienced a destructive drought in the spring and summer of 1986.

All signs point to the beginning of the Scenario as shown to me first as a child and then in the Faraday copper cage as an adult. The winds of change are in the headlines of newspapers all around the globe. No longer is speaking about earthquakes and volcanoes, heat waves and droughts, considered doom and gloom. They are facts of life. The Ogatta group told us the transitions and changes would not come in "one big boom." They said that for those who would but open their eyes, the signs of change would be abundant. "Tell them to prepare," they urged Dick and me. And we, through S.T.A.R. Foundation, are prepared to help others through the changes and devastation, should they find their way to us. We have stored food, medical supplies, and clothing to help one hundred people through a one-year period. It is not our intention that people come and stay, but rather that people come and go, be refreshed and refurbished, and sent on their way. Hopefully, they will then do the same for others who need help. We feel, in the words of the Ogattans, that we are "right on target!"

Once Dick asked Tauri what the Earth's population would be like after the destruction. Tauri answered, "You can look at an island with a palm tree on it and coconuts hanging down and monkeys swinging from the branches. Right across from the island there can be a tidal wave, and the coconuts will not move and the palm tree will sway in the breeze and be untouched.

"So will this be. Small islands of people remain untouched while huge areas can be decimated."

The Ogattans say the storms are coming. Yes, even here, in restful Reisha Way, I look out my window and see those storm clouds gathering . . .

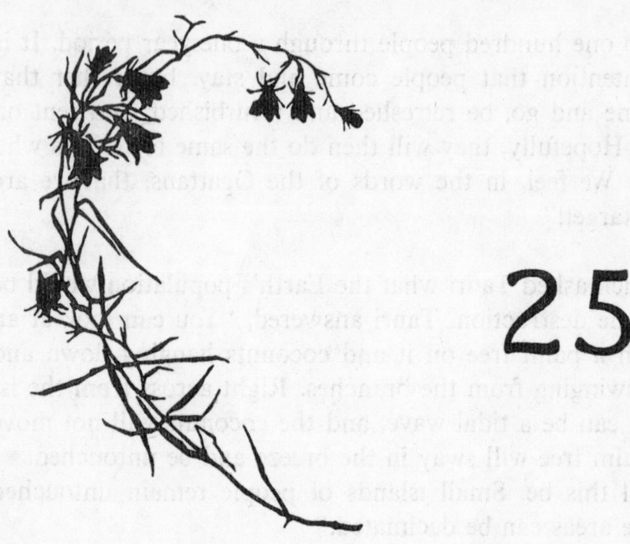

25

IF YOU CAST a fish line into the cosmic ocean, do you really expect our Space Elders to bite on your hook? Is it not more rational to think that they would visit us at a time and place of their own choosing, on their own terms, and with more advanced technology?

Anybody who reads a newspaper or goes to movies knows about UFOs. Stories of bright lights in the sky, disc-shaped vehicles in the daylight, and encounters on the ground have fascinated the world public and given rise to endless controversy. Scientists have mostly been skeptical, but few of them have actually bothered to investigate the reports. Most of those who have, such as the late Northwestern University astronomer J. Allen Hynek (whom Dick and I met in Chicago and found a delightful man), have concluded that something is going on—alien visitation, some are bold enough to suggest.

Hundreds of books, thousands of magazine articles, and tens of thousands of newspaper clippings attest to the persistence of UFOs and UFO sightings. The world is gradually waking up to the reality of visitors from other worlds. This was a reality, as we've seen, that I was aware of at a very early age, and it is a reality that I live with every day. And soon it will be an inescapable reality for everybody.

One day a few years ago, Tauri made us aware of just how long they have been observing our planet. She was giving us some fascinating data about the Cherokee Indians who lived in the mountains of Georgia and North Carolina before the settlers arrived and took their lands. When Dick asked how she could possibly know about it, Tauri replied, "We've been observing your little planet for thousands of years." Dick asked, "Have the gattae from other civilizations been observing our planet for that long too?" Tauri answered, "I do not know how long other civilizations have been observing your tiny planet, but I do know that we have not been the only ones." She went on to correct Dick. "The gattae is the name we give *our* spacecraft, Dick. I do not know what all the others call *their* craft." She brimmed with amusement and added, "I do know that you humans lump all of them under one name: 'UFOs'!" So, UFOs have been part of our unacknowledged landscape for a lot longer than we might suspect.

Let's take a brief diversion into history to look at UFOs as people have experienced them—and also at the very interesting (but little-known) story of what our government knows about extraterrestrials and when it learned about them. Be prepared to be surprised.

Something visited Brazil on May 19, 1986. The incident began in the early evening, when the São Paulo radar station picked up an unknown object on the screen. The operators notified the occupants of a two-engine executive plane, a Xingu, which was about to land, and they saw a "dancing point in the sky" in the area of the sky indicated by the radar. The pilot of the plane was a well-known Brazilian, Colonel Osires Silva, who had just been appointed head of his country's state-owned oil company.

With Osires Silva was a veteran airline pilot, Commander Alcir Pereira da Silva. The UFO as he described it was "brighter than a star, emitting a constant red orange light." The light went off, coming on again a few seconds later when the object was at another location. The two pilots chased the UFO for half an hour before giving up.

Meanwhile, with this and other unknown objects showing up on both civilian and military radar screens in the area, Brazilian Air Force jets were scrambled from bases at Santa Cruz and Anapolis. Over the next four hours they chased elusive aerial phenomena whose speeds considerably outdistanced those the earthly aircraft were able to attain. Also, the UFOs—there were about a dozen of them—were executing sharp, right-angle turns and other incredible maneuvers. By midnight they were gone.

Soon afterward the Air Force allowed those involved in the episode to hold a press conference in which they freely described what they had seen. One of the traffic controllers, Lieutenant Valdecir Fernando Coehlo, declared, "In my fourteen years of experience as a radar operator, I never saw anything like this."

The military announced it was going to conduct an in-depth investigation. Brazil's Air Minister, Brigadier Octavio Julio Moreira Lima, said the reports were being taken very seriously. "Radar is not subject to optical illusions," he stated. "The radar echoes are due to solid objects or to massive clouds, which were not present that night."

Such openness about UFOs is not the way official bodies usually deal with the problem. In our own country, things have been handled very differently.

The UFO age began here on June 24, 1947, when a private pilot named Kenneth Arnold reported seeing nine craftlike objects flying in formation over Mount Rainier. When he said their movement reminded him of saucers skipping across water, an enterprising reporter invented the unfortunate term "flying saucers." In the days and weeks to follow, many other Americans from all walks of life reported seeing strange shapes in the sky.

According to the official history—the one that we've been told about and are supposed to believe—the Air Force began a small UFO project, code-named Sign, to investigate the reports. Early on, basing their judgment on these sighting reports, Sign investigators suspected that the "flying discs" were extraterrestrial spacecraft. In 1948 they forwarded their conclusions in an "Estimate of the Situation" to the Air Force Chief of Staff, General Hoyt S. Vandenberg, who rejected the notion and ordered that all copies of the document be burned. The Air Force then embarked on a campaign of UFO debunking under two subsequent UFO projects, Grudge and Blue Book. In 1969 Blue Book was closed and the Air Force announced that it would no longer investigate UFO reports.

In recent years, as civilian researchers have studied official documents and interviewed persons close to the government agencies responsible, an entirely different picture of what really happened has emerged. The situation now coming to light has been described by nuclear scientist and UFO investigator Stanton Friedman as a "Cosmic Watergate," an expression I thought I had coined in the 1970s.

The key event, the investigators say, happened in early July 1947, just over a week after Arnold's sighting. On the evening of July 2, residents of Roswell, New Mexico, saw a glowing disc-shaped object pass low overhead, heading toward the northwest. That night, in a remote ranch area seventy-five miles northwest of Roswell, local people heard what sounded like an explosion in the sky. Although the "explosion" took place in the midst of a blinding rainstorm (perhaps explaining why no one rushed outside to check its cause), witnesses were later to insist it sounded nothing like thunder.

The following morning, rancher Mac Brazel and two of his children discovered a great quantity of mysterious material scattered over his property. It was a metallic substance, tough yet oddly light, with peculiar, hieroglyphic-like writing on it. There was also a quantity of something that looked like brown "parchment," thin but extremely strong.

Brazel, who had no phone, did not report the discovery until a few days later. Investigators from the Army Air Force base at Roswell rushed to the scene, collected all the material and threatened all who knew of the incident, including local reporters, to remain silent. Secrecy was so rigidly enforced that a press wire story being transmitted out of Albuquerque was interrupted with a warning that it must go no farther. Brazel was held incommunicado for nearly a week afterward.

The material was flown to Eighth Air Force Headquarters at Carswell Air Force Base in Fort Worth, Texas, where General Roger M. Ramey invented a cover story claiming that the "object" was only a balloon. Meanwhile the material was secretly flown, under armed guard, to Wright Field in Dayton, Ohio. (Wright Field was soon to become Wright-Patterson Air Force Base, where the Air Force's UFO projects were headquartered.) The present whereabouts of the material are not known.

In the three decades after the Roswell incident, rumors circulated that the Air Force possessed the remains of crashed UFOs, but the stories proved unverifiable. Even UFO researchers thought them as little more than space-age tall tales.

Then in the mid-1970s Friedman and William Moore, after getting a tip from a reliable source, began a dogged pursuit of the few leads in the Roswell story. Since then they have interviewed over ninety persons who were directly or indirectly involved in the episode. They have learned that the object was recognized almost immediately as something extraordinary and that the investigators soon concluded it was a vehicle from another solar system.

Another student of the U.S. Government UFO cover-up is Bruce Maccabee, who works professionally as an optical physicist employed by the Naval Surface Weapons Laboratory. In recent years Dr. Maccabee has studied thousands of official documents and interviewed dozens of individuals privy to the secrets of official involvement with the UFO phenomenon. Maccabee is convinced that the low-level officers involved in the publicly visible projects such as Sign, Grudge, and Blue Book were kept completely in the dark about the truth. In effect, they served as unwitting participants in the cover-up.

"The Air Force knew by the middle of July 1947," he writes, "that saucers were real and not man-made. Furthermore, it is not unreasonable to add the corollary that the Air Force knew that the technology represented by the disc [recovered in New Mexico] . . . was so far beyond our own that it could not be understood immediately. Instead, it would take years of research in advanced physics to understand how a disc worked. Moreover, clearly whoever has discs 'wins' in a military sense. Therefore it would become necessary to treat the disc as a military secret. This would mean containing all information about it within some small group. The military agencies best equipped for containing information are the intelligence agencies. Therefore the disc would be placed in the custody of an intelligence arm of the Air Force."

An internal Air Force memorandum, dated October 20, 1969, confirms that Blue Book was effectively removed from the real UFO investigation. The memorandum, written by Brigadier General C. H. Bolender and obtained years later under the Freedom of Information Act, states that "reports . . . which could affect national security . . . are not part of the Blue Book system . . . [and are handled through the standard Air Force procedures designed for this purpose]."

Maccabee concludes from his own investigation that a secret group reports directly to the President, Secretary of Defense, and the Joint Chiefs of Staff. It bypassed the public UFO projects, which were given "civilian/military verbal reports while the top Air Force generals maintain[ed] absolute secrecy about the real thing. That way they got to collect data which might have been useful without having to reveal what they knew. To the outside world it looked as if the Air Force was fulfilling its duty to investigate unknowns in the sky but with little hope of finding anything."

On September 15, 1950, scientists from the Canadian Embassy staff met physicist Robert Sarbacher at his office in the Department of Defense's Research and Development Board. Nearly thirty years later a memo detailing what Sarbacher said in that meeting came to light. The scientists had asked him if the U.S. Government had physical remains of UFOs. Sarbacher said yes. According to the memo, written by a Canadian government engineer named Wilbert B. Smith, he also said:

The matter is the most highly classified subject in the United States Government, rating higher even than the H-bomb.

Flying saucers exist.

Their modus operandi is unknown but concentrated effort is being made by a small group headed by Dr. Vannevar Bush.

The entire matter is considered by the United States authorities to be of tremendous significance.

In 1983, not long after Smith's memo came to light, Sarbacher was located at the Florida address listed in his *Who's Who in America* entry—over three inches of tiny print detailing an extraordinary career in science, government, and business. Along with many other impressive professional achievements, Sarbacher was dean of the graduate school at the Georgia Institute of Technology and served as a consultant for the Oak Ridge Institute for Nuclear Studies. His *Encyclopedia Dictionary of Electronics and Engineering* is considered an essential scientific text. He directed the General Sciences Corporation and the Union Life Insurance Company. He invented a landing system used by airliners all over the world. In other words, he could not be written off as "just another flying-saucer nut."

Sarbacher confirmed that our government possesses the remains of UFOs, which he said were believed to be vehicles from another solar system. These remains, he reported, were stored, at least in the early 1950s, at Wright-Patterson AFB.

"Certain materials reported to have come from flying-saucer crashes were extremely light and very tough," he wrote to a UFO researcher, apparently referring to the Roswell material. "Instruments or people operating these machines were also of very light weight, sufficient to withstand the tremendous deceleration and acceleration associated with their machinery . . .

"I still do not know why the high order of classification has been given and why the denial of the existence of these devices."

Subsequently Sarbacher was interviewed in person by Stanton Friedman. Sarbacher died on July 26, 1986.

Other knowledgeable individuals, insisting that their identities be protected, have told Maccabee, Friedman, Moore, and others the same incredible story.

It is now believed that the above-top-secret group privy to the government's most classified UFO secrets was (and may still be) called MJ-12 (rumored to be short for "Majestic 12"), made up of elite scientists and military leaders. The first head of the group, Vannevar Bush, was the President's chief science consultant. Among its members were James Forrestal, Secretary of Defense in the early years of the Truman administration; Roscoe H. Hillenkoetter, the first CIA director; and Sidney Souers, first executive secretary of the National Security Council.

In later years Admiral Hillenkoetter was to go public with a declaration, reported in the New York *Times* on February 28, 1960, that "behind the scenes, high-ranking Air Force officers are soberly concerned about UFOs. But, through official secrecy and ridicule, many citizens are led to believe the unknown flying objects are nonsense." Hillenkoetter never revealed the UFO secrets, most dramatically those relating to the actual recovery of a craft at Roswell, to which he was privy, however. Maccabee believes that Hillenkoetter opposed the policy of secrecy but was unwilling to violate his own oath to remain silent.

In the summer of 1987 the MJ-12 story made headlines all around the world when two UFO researchers, William Moore and Timothy Good of England, released a nine-page document with explosive contents. Moore and Good were separately given the document, supposedly a National Security Council briefing paper dated November 18, 1952, by anonymous sources with official connections. The document is said to have been written by Admiral Hillenkoetter, and it tells President-elect Eisenhower that the U.S. Government has the remains of two craft that "do not originate in any country on Earth."

The paper describes the Roswell incident and adds that the bodies of "four small humanlike beings . . . badly decomposed due to action by predators" were found some distance from the crash site. They "had apparently ejected from the craft at some point before it exploded." The paper also mentions another incident which occurred in December 1950, when a UFO crashed near the Texas-Mexico border, but "by the time a research team arrived, what remained of the object had been almost totally incinerated."

The document says MJ-12 is a "TOP SECRET Research and Development/Intelligence operation responsible directly and only to the President of the United States." Its members included Admiral Hillenkoetter, Dr. Bush, Secretary Forrestal, Air Force General Nathan Twining, and Harvard University astronomer Donald H. Menzel (who was publicly known as a UFO debunker).

The document was discussed in the New York *Times* and on ABC-TV's "Nightline," and created a lot of excitement, but nobody knows yet if it's real or fake. If it is a fake, it's a good one. If it isn't fake, it's what politicians call a "smoking gun."

The evidence and controversy surrounding the Cosmic Watergate continue, and it is likely that we will be hearing a great deal more about it in times to come.

UFOs continue to be seen all over the world, of course, and these days almost everyone has his own UFO story to tell. My favorite one was told to Dick and me in 1984 prior to giving a lecture in Johannesburg, South Africa. We were on safari to Botswana (where the movie *The Gods Must Be Crazy* was filmed). There two displaced and well-educated Rhodesians pulled us aside to talk about our E.T. connections. They related this event, which they said occurred while they were still living in Zimbabwe:

"A huge UFO landed," they said, "and hundreds of people gathered to see the craft. Entities came out of the ship and were quietly and respectfully saluted by everyone present. We just knew that they came in peace and would come back some day."

Then the two Rhodesians sadly related another encounter. After they left their homeland and relocated in Botswana, they were thrilled to see a craft hovering overhead.

In Botswana, however, the reception was entirely different. They told us, "Military came at the craft with gunfire, and people screamed and fled in panic and fear." They doubted that E.T.s would ever return after such hostility. "Why should they come back?" they lamented. "In Zimbabwe they were met with love . . . and here they were met with fear."

I think that Botswana will have a long, long wait for another visit.

A famous "close encounter of the third kind" (as Dr. Hynek called reports of encounters with UFO occupants) occurred late in June 1959 in another remote location, the village of Boianai, Papua New Guinea. There, early in the evening of the twenty-sixth, thirty-eight persons, one of them an Anglican missionary from Australia, the Reverend William Booth Gill, saw a large disc-shaped object with four legs hover overhead. On top of the craft witnesses saw four illuminated humanlike figures seeming to be "doing something on deck," in Gill's words. An hour later the object was lost to view in gathering clouds.

At six o'clock the following evening the UFO and its occupants returned, to resume the same enigmatic task with which they had been engaged the night before. This time Gill and a dozen companions waved and shouted to the "men," trying to get them to land their ship and come to dinner with them. The beings waved back for a minute or two, then resumed their work.

Father Gill and the other witnesses all signed a statement attesting to their incredible experience. Some years later Dr. Hynek met Gill in Australia and subsequently, in the company of one of Gill's missionary colleagues, made his way to Boianai, where he interviewed half a dozen of the native witnesses. Although this was fourteen years after the sighting, Hynek said, "I came away with the impression that, whatever the event was, it must have impressed the heck out of them to have remembered it as vividly as they did. There was never any question on their part that 'maybe it happened, maybe it didn't happen'—it *did* happen. They were quite sure of that."

Sightings of UFOs are extremely common. A 1978 Gallup Poll revealed that thirteen million Americans believed they had seen UFOs. Since then, I'm sure, the figure is considerably higher.

In early January 1987 the newspapers were full of accounts of a spectacular sighting which took place on November 17, 1986, although it did not come to light until a month and a half later, when a relative of one of the witnesses tipped off the press.

On the evening in question Japan Air Lines Flight 1628 was on its way to Anchorage, Alaska, from Reykjavik, when pilot Kenjyu Terauchi, a forty-seven-year-old veteran, and two crewmen spotted flashing lights moving alongside them. At the time their 747 cargo plane was passing over the Beaufort Sea off the north coast of Alaska.

The lights were about eight miles away, matching the plane's altitude of thirty-five thousand feet. Terauchi radioed the Federal Aviation Administration headquarters in Anchorage and asked permission to descend to thirty-one thousand feet. Permission granted, he did so, only to find the lights "descending in formation," he reported, with his aircraft. When he turned his plane in a 360-degree circle, the lights followed him.

At one point the men aboard the plane got a good look at what they were seeing. There were in fact three objects: two lights about eight feet across and a huge walnut-shaped craft the length of two aircraft carriers. The large object had a wide flat rim and "bulges" above and below it. There was no question it was there: it was on the cockpit's weather radar. Still, just to be sure, Terauchi dimmed the lights in the plane to make sure he and his companions were seeing something that was genuinely out there, not just reflecting on the windows. Even with the cabin lights out, the object was there.

The UFOs followed the plane for almost an hour before disappearing in the direction of Canada. All the while, the witnesses reported, the objects flanked each other, flashing a brilliant pattern of yellow, amber, and green lights.

When the plane landed in Anchorage, FAA personnel interviewed the crew and found them, in an FAA spokesman's words, "professional, rational, well-trained people." The spokesman said of their sighting, "It's a mystery."

Despite many thousands of sightings from sane, reputable, and often trained observers, most of the scientific establishment chooses to dismiss the UFO phenomenon out of hand, refusing even to consider the growing evidence. For a time it was willing to investigate the possibility of extraterrestrial life—at a safe distance—through monitoring of signals from deep space with radio telescopes. This enterprise, known as SETI (Search for Extraterrestrial Intelligence), was championed by such prominent astronomers as Carl Sagan and Frank Drake. Now, however, even it has fallen into disrepute.

A few years ago, when NASA asked for fifteen million dollars for its SETI project, Senator William Proxmire of Wisconsin gave the agency his notorious Golden Fleece award. Recently Tulane University astrophysicist Frank Tipler called SETI a "boondoggle" and accused those involved with it of being "like evangelicals—this is a religion." Dr. Tipler is one of a growing number of scientists who believe intelligent life is confined to the Earth. "Most leading experts in evolutionary biology," he says, "contend that the Earth is probably unique in harboring intelligence, at least amongst the planets of our galaxy."

Dr. Carl Sagan has written that contact with extraterrestrials is essential for humanity because such beings may offer "detailed prescription for the avoidance of technological disaster."

The SETI controversy doesn't interest me at all, except as an example of human beings' capacity for blindness and self-delusion. After all, I personally have no need to search for what I know is there—what, in fact, I have already found.

I rode on a spacecraft—gattae—when I was small, and I observed others as an adult at close range both in Ossining and at home on Dick's birthday. Why spend valuable time with UFO buffs proving they are real, or with debunkers wearing blinders proving they are imaginary. But it is interesting and encouraging to observe that Americans are ahead of the scientists on this issue. A 1985 Gallup poll shows that 47 percent of the American people believe there is intelligent life on other planets. Forty-nine percent agree that "the search for such life is a good use for research money." What was especially fascinating to me was that the more educated the respondent, the more likely he was to believe in the existence of extraterrestrials. The most skeptical group consisted of high-school dropouts!

Even as governments maintain pointless secrecy about extraterrestrial visitation, and scientists foolishly deny its very possibility, the reality of life elsewhere is becoming ever more apparent to the people of our world.

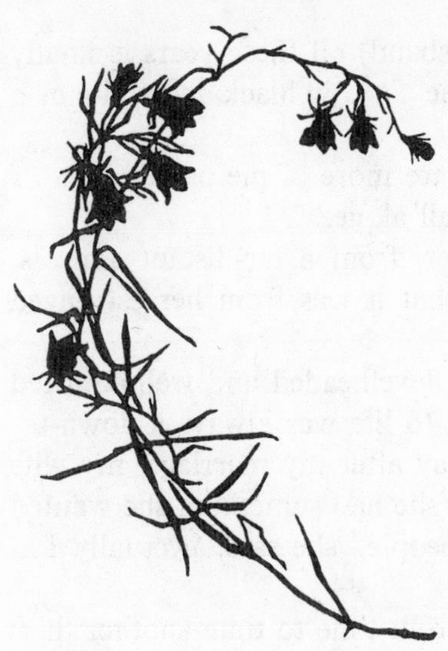

26

ONE MANIFESTATION of the growing awareness of other intelligences is the growing incidence of channeling throughout the world.

Dick and I saw plenty of evidence of this after my book *On a Slide of Light* came out. We got a flood of letters from people expressing astonishment and relief in finding they were not alone.

I remember especially well two particular letters. The first was from a woman named Judy:

"Thanking you for writing your book . . . Where have you been all my life? . . . I have been trying for the last fifteen to twenty years to connect my being to why I'm not like others; why what abilities I have are normal to me and not to others; and why I have always looked to space, somewhere, as my home. I have read tons of books . . . chased countless rainbows . . . considered myself a nut. I am here . . . I see a home unlike here. I see the normal day . . . streets . . . trees . . . I see the aftereffects of destruction. I was really at my wits' end. I had great hopes once . . . but . . . a desperate alien/human person never gives up looking for the 'mother ship.' Everything that I have been telling Robert (my husband) all these years is finally published by someone who isn't me . . . in black and white by a nationally prestigious publisher.

"I kept yelling, 'I know there are more of me out there . . . where are they? . . . I can't be all alone.' "

A few days later another letter, from a far-distant address, arrived, and it became obvious that it was from her estranged husband:

"I am in every way a normal, levelheaded and well-adjusted person. In the past my approach to life was always a down-to-earth, nuts-and-bolts way. One day after my marriage, my wife approached me nervously, saying she had something she wanted to tell me. 'I am not like other people,' she said. 'Actually I'm two people.'

"She went on to explain how from time to time another 'her' inhabits her body. The other 'her' lives on a planet called Lomar in the Pleiades constellation. Through this other person she receives formulas for propulsion systems . . . theories on something called 'photonic propulsion.'

"She looks out the window of the apartment and instead of seeing the building across the street, she sees a futuristic city. [As she walks] downtown, for a moment the town will be gone and she is surrounded by total desolation. There have been instances of objects materializing and dematerializing off her desk.

"At first I tried to be open-minded about all of this, but eventually it wore me down. Finally I couldn't take it anymore and we separated.

"Your book floored me. I was stunned to discover that someone else had experienced things that I thought were manifestations of my wife's unique 'neurosis.' Whom do I turn to for help? Can you help?"

Later we met with this couple who was attempting a reconciliation. We spent a few hours with them, trying to comfort them and offer advice on how to handle the channeling experience. Judy, who shares the channel with an entity named Zun, asks and is given answers to diverse questions, from photonic propulsion systems to earthquakes and other future global events. She said she felt "fragmented" and Bob said he was "confused" about who she really was.

Judy is among the many awakening to the coming changes. Many people are being prepared to serve as channels for information from more advanced civilizations.

My book produced a shock of recognition for a number of these individuals. One of them, a woman from Hawaii, wrote, "I heard your message and a few notes of music played within me." An Arizonian related, "It is not clear to me what I could do or how I would fit in, but I have been directed in the dream state to 'help allay the fears of mankind before and during the upcoming landings.' " A Californian said, "I was so relieved to find your book and discover that I was not alone. I am conscious of many synchronicities in my life and the feeling of a 'mission' I cannot remember." A Canadian told me, "I am a man who has had the same experiences as you. Though I never hid it, the results made me feel like a round peg in a square hole. It can be very lonely." A Ph.D. from Georgia stated, "I have had similar experiences these past two years but unfortunately I must be careful about telling of these experiences. I could lose my grant and be labeled 'unstable.' That's the kind of academic environment I live in."

Every summer, people who channel information from supposedly extraterrestrial sources meet in Laramie, on the campus of the University of Wyoming, to attend the annual gathering of the Rocky Mountain Conference on UFO Investigation. These "contactees" all report that the human race is undergoing a "raising of vibrations" in preparation for great Earth changes and the arrival of space people who will help usher in a new age.

The man behind these conferences is psychologist R. Leo Sprinkle, who for years before organizing them had been corresponding with channels. They all wanted to know "Why me?" Dr. Sprinkle thought that maybe they could find an answer to that question if they had a place to meet each other and to speak freely. In 1980 the first conference was held. Each year more and more people have been attracted to the gatherings.

In his observation, Dr. Sprinkle says, the stories he hears are consistent, "and the people who are telling the stories come from all walks of life and from all over the world. These experiences have tremendous effects on their lives; yet most of them don't have anybody to talk to about it. I think these people deserve to be heard."

He and his colleague Dr. June Parnell have conducted psychological studies of over two hundred channels and found that, contrary to the stereotypes about "nuts," they are perfectly normal human beings.

At one of these conferences a channel named Ann Canary summed up what she has learned from her long interaction with extraterrestrial intelligences:

"After many years, I now realize and know that my own transformation was not and is not a single experience here on Earth. There are literally hundreds if not thousands of people who have experienced this metamorphosis. Our numbers are growing yearly and we are beginning to locate and communicate with each other. An alien invasion has already occurred on Earth. The conquering power is not military or technological/economic superiority. It is a revolution in consciousness and spiritual knowing that has been implanted within the minds of thousands of people all over the world. The future of this world is passing into the hands of these people.

"Those of us who have been contacted no longer serve the old orders. We fear nothing . . . We are here—now! We walk among you daily—we pass you on the streets, stand next to you in the elevators, and you see little of what is moving daily closer to its completion. We are among you—and our force is the force of mind governed by morality and an ethical code that upon Earth is incomprehensible."

The channeling phenomenon is becoming so widespread that even the mainstream media are taking note. On Sunday, November 16, 1986, no less than the august New York *Times* gave front-page coverage to the entity Ramtha, who channels through a Yelm, Washington woman named J. Z. Knight. Ramtha warns of coming Earth changes and speaks to the urgent need for mankind to expand its consciousness in order to deal with new cosmic realities. The message is very familiar.

I suspect, however, that the channeling phenomenon has been around for a long time, influencing human development in a positive way. Take, for example, some curious aspects of that allegedly human ability we call "genius."

In the Broadway show and subsequent film *Amadeus,* author Peter Shaffer depicts Wolfgang Amadeus Mozart as being "otherworldly." He recounts how Mozart used to hear entire compositions in his head and then simply trace the instruments' parts and commit them to paper. One of the show's finest moments involves the discovery of a Mozart transcript by his contemporary Antonio Salieri. When Salieri sees the sheet of music—devoid of a single erasure mark—he concludes that Mozart is a "genius" with a "direct communication to God."

It is certainly intriguing to read Mozart's own description of the way in which he formulated his music. In his *Life of Mozart,* biographer Edward Holmes quotes this revealing letter written by Mozart:

"When I am, as it were, completely myself, entirely alone and of good cheer . . . it is on such occasions that my ideas flow best and most abundantly. Whence and how they come, I know not; nor can I force them. Those ideas that please me I retain in memory, and am accustomed, as I have been told, to hum to myself. All this fires my soul, and, provided I am not disturbed, my subject enlarges itself, becomes methodized and defined, and the whole, though it be long, stands almost complete and finished in my mind, so that I can survey it, like a fine picture, or a beautiful statue, at a glance. Nor do I hear in my imagination the parts successively, but I hear them, as it were, all at once."

And Mozart heard them often. His life as a composer began when he was a mere five years old. Before his death at thirty-five, he composed more than six hundred musical works—operas, sonatas, concertos, and more than forty-one symphonies—which rank among the great cultural treasures of the human race.

The "genius" of Yugoslav-born scientist Nikola Tesla—the only scientist ever to refuse a Nobel Prize—is described in much the same way. If he thought of any object, it would appear before him, exhibiting three-dimensional properties. So vivid and tangible did these visions appear that it was usually difficult for Tesla "to distinguish between vision and reality," his biographer John J. O'Neill notes. Discoveries and inventions played out in Tesla's head. He built mental constructs with meticulous care, and precisely worked out size, strength, design, and material. He said he allowed these mental machines to run for extended periods of time so that he could examine them thoroughly for signs of wear! Tesla would then assemble the required materials and construct his models without hesitation or mistake.

Much of what Tesla developed was before its time and went unappreciated. Tesla solved the world's energy crisis in the early 1900s, long before the world even knew there was such a problem. He determined that the electrical potential of nondepletable energy between the Earth and the upper atmosphere was some two billion volts. He then formulated a system of oscillating this static reserve of electrical energy at a specific frequency in order to release energy for practical purposes. The "Tesla frequency," long lost, only now is the subject of serious scientific research in the United States and elsewhere.

It is tempting to speculate that both Mozart's and Tesla's "genius" was aided by the wisdom of advanced civilizations. Perhaps both men were channels. It is not generally known that Tesla believed much of his scientific information came from extraterrestrials.

Just as the Ogatta group trained me to communicate—to trumpet the voice and scribe the pen—so too are many individuals being trained to receive the advanced technology that will be required to rebuild society after the changes have taken place. We have met some of the brave men and women who work in areas of science and technology for which their only reward is ridicule from an entrenched peer group. But undaunted, these New Age scientists pursue their vital work.

With the help of the Ogattans and the other benign extraterrestrial civilizations, mankind will succeed in spite of itself. When Bucky Fuller said "Man is not meant to fail," the Ogatta group nodded in agreement.

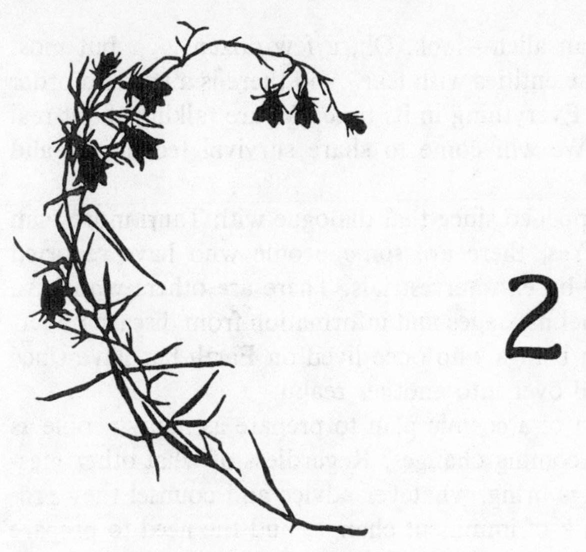

27

WHEN THE OGATTA GROUP first contacted me again, at the end of 1976, they told me I was to allay the fears of people when they came.

"Tell them that we come in peace to help in their time of transition, in their time of greatest need," the Ogattans said. It seemed like an impossible task. How could we assuage this fear of alien, albeit benign visitors when their very existence was not acknowledged? Were they saying to me, in effect, that I was to try to allay fear of the unknown?

Why did they have to communicate through channels anyway? Why didn't they just come and make themselves known to mankind and get their messages out themselves? Tauri gave this answer:

"In using channels, we use less energy. The vibration is lower. If we were to come and sit next to you, you could not handle that vibration if you were not prepared. The energy levels are too great for your fragile human frames. You do not want good people 'blown out' because they cannot handle those vibrations. Anyway, I doubt at this point that many are ready to see entities of a different—an alien—look. Oh, a few dozen . . . but most would greet these entities with fear. And there is a law and order in the universe. Everything in its time. We are talking about real survival, now. We will come to share survival techniques and technologies."

Much has happened since that dialogue with Tauri more than a decade ago. Yes, there are some people who have reported being contacted by extraterrestrials. There are others who have started to channel messages and information from discarnate terrestrials, human beings who once lived on Earth but have since died and crossed over into another realm.

Is this all part of a cosmic plan to prepare as many people as possible for the coming changes? Regardless of what other messages these beings bring, whatever advice and counsel they propose, they all talk of imminent changes and the need to prepare for them as best we can. In my opinion, these are the only words to take to heart.

Actress Shirley MacLaine went "out on a limb" in her books and television miniseries. When she speaks of "consciousness-raising" and "spiritual attunement," she is also talking about preparedness for the new vibrations that are coming in. She is a prominent spokeswoman for New Age thinking through heightened awareness.

We have dear close friends—among them Andrija Puharich, Tom Beardon, Norman Shealy, Harold Sherman, and Ruth Montgomery—who have authored many books about coming changes and stepped-up vibrations. The more that the message is put out there, the easier my mission becomes.

There are, however, some voices with disturbing messages. What they report is so totally different from my own experience that I admit I have a hard time understanding it. I refer to the messages of fear associated with "abductees" who tell of being taken, against their will, aboard spacecraft, where they are subjected to painful biological tests and probes. The memory of the event is then wiped from their minds, to reemerge later through either hypnotic probing or spontaneous recall.

The suffering these people experience is very real. Psychologists who have studied abductees say they have the psychological profiles of victims of criminal assault. Dr. Elizabeth Slater, a psychologist from New York City, says the typical abductee is like "the rape victim, who has been violated most brutally but somehow becomes tainted by virtue of the crime against her"; society declares that UFO abductions cannot occur and so ridicules those who have such experiences, which only adds to their suffering.

One abductee, a well-known sci-fi novelist, says that his experiences were terrifying; yet "my impression is that these people, if they exist, are more than a little afraid of us: They are deeply afraid." He describes the creatures as 'buglike' and refers to them as aliens; aliens who abduct humans against their free will, and inflict physical pain in examination.

It bothers me very much that someone's first exposure to extraterrestrial life might be the view presented by this abductee/author. A view of fear and of anguish. Given our society's way of looking at the dark side of things, it is disturbing that this view of extraterrestrials will be taken as the correct one. It makes my work of "allaying the fears when they come" a more difficult task. It is a step backward for true understanding.

It bothered Dick also. At the first opportunity he brought his upset to Tauri. The resulting conversation follows:

TAURI: When your scientists seek laboratory confirmation of theories and ideas, they use specimens, mice, rats, and other guinea pigs in their work. They seek to conduct their experiments in the most human way they can, but also the most productive and efficient. They attempt to remain totally detached and objective in their approach, removing themselves from emotional involvement. Their end goal is to enrich the store of knowledge in the area in which they are working. Do you understand this, Dick?

DICK: Yes.

TAURI: If you understand this then you will have no trouble understanding a civilization that sends its best scientists to study areas in which their knowledge is sparse.

DICK: But the knowledge of man is available in the cosmos in far greater detail than their cursory probes can provide.

TAURI: Yes, it is, but only for those who can tap into it.

DICK: Can't they?

TAURI: Dick! We have spoken many times about *technological* advancement not being spiritual or moral advancement. These civilizations can travel in the cosmos, but they are no further advanced in their other development than mankind. Need I give you examples of these civilizations?

DICK: No. I am fully aware of what you say.

TAURI: Now let me tell you some things about these civilizations. They send their very best scientists to learn the ways on a planet they probe. On Earth they study plants, insects, animals, and Man. They go to great lengths *not* to harm or frighten any human with whom they work. They view Man as they would other specimens they study, and try to respect the "free will" aspects within this context. While there are a few legitimate abductees, there are not nearly as many as you would think. Most who report such experiences suffer from "head noises!" Now that you see the public airing this activity is receiving, you will better understand Greta's assignment of "allaying the fears." While you may think that the study of man violates free will, they are much gentler than your own kind when they use man as an object of study. You are aware of human studies that use man as guinea pigs without their knowledge and against their free will?

DICK: Yes, unfortunately I am, Tauri.

Tauri then shifted the conversation to another topic and the subject of abductees was closed. Our understanding of the abductee phenomenon was greatly expanded. These clinical beings operate their knowledge-collecting probes (as do *our* scientists) from a totally objective approach. They do not seek to be controversial figures or "negative forces" on our planet. They're just not advanced enough to tap into the available cosmic knowledge. Well! Neither are we. Sometime in the future, when we become able to explore distant worlds, we too may fall into the category of abductors seeking to learn about life on a distant planet. I hope that we remember the experiences being written about by our human abductees and seek the assistance of the many on the planet who would deem it an honor to be examined by an extraterrestrial civilization.

Let me tell you of another conversation that Dick had with Tauri when reports of "Bigfoot" creatures abounded in the mid- to late 1970s.

"Where are all these big hairy creatures coming from?" Dick wanted to know.

"They are from a planet called Bergan," Tauri said. "Miserable place. I haven't been there, but I know. They have no music and they have no light as we know light. They are hairy and very, verrrry peculiar looking! In your mythology they were known by the funny word 'yeti.' They are physically very big and yes, they can be pretty frightening to the humans."

"But how do they get here?"

"They come in a materializing (and dematerializing) way."

"Isn't that pretty advanced stuff?"

"Advanced scientifically . . . technologically . . . yes. Advanced mentally . . . no! There's a difference, you know. Don't ever deify beings from other planets just because they can do things that you humans cannot. Keep it light! Some things that others can do appear wondrous only by your limited definitions and technology. On their dimensions these feats are a way of life, nothing more. I will tell you that, for most civilizations that live outside planet Earth, dematerialization is just a normal way of existence.

"Now, these Bergans are not good for very much but they can materialize. Just because you humans haven't linked into the way to dematerialize yourselves doesn't mean it's such a wonderful thing to do. Sometimes I think they [Bergans] have small brains in their big bodies. They're pretty useless. They eat barks of trees . . . bark and tree stuff. But they are harmless and you have nothing to fear from them, even though they might appear scary to look at if you don't know what they are."

Without wanting to belittle the entities that abduct human beings against their will, I can only place the level of their evolution and understanding in the same general category with the Bergans. Advanced extraterrestrials have no need to make biological forays onto our planet. That knowledge is available to them in far greater detail than any abduction examinations can possibly provide. Frightening people just doesn't fit into our understanding of the cosmos. As Tauri says:

"There is a law and order in the universe, and laws are not meant to be broken. We have used the words 'free will' so much that perhaps you lose sight of what they really mean. You have total free will in what you choose to do with your time . . . with your mind . . . with your body . . . with your commitment. There is a time that we of the Ogatta group step back and watch . . . and we wait . . . and we listen . . . and we evaluate. Sometimes we wish we could change the free will, but we don't. And other times, we say 'bravo!' "

Dick and Tauri have also discussed the disappearances that take place in an area that has come to be known as the Bermuda Triangle. The explanation is interesting:

"There is a group that has a craft, a spaceship, not too far from that Bermuda Triangle," Tauri said. "When they wish to make themselves known, they do. Their hands, their vibrations, and their harmonics are capable of dematerializing what comes in the wake of those bands. That's not so wonderful. Everybody can do that except humans on planet Earth."

Dick asked, "When they dematerialize these ships and planes with the people on them, where do they materialize them again? The people, I mean."

"They simply go back to their home base. Anybody who has disappeared in the Bermuda Triangle was meant to go back to their own home base. They each had a mission, and it was accomplished, and that was the climax. The end of the mission. They were ready to go back. Some of them knew it consciously and some did not."

"And the physical craft?"

"They don't have any meaning. They are left in atoms and never assembled again."

"Are they from one of the planets that will be coming to help us in our time of transition?"

"It won't be too long before that will come to light. But that should not come through me. But I will tell you this: Do not feel too sorry for anyone who 'disappeared.' They were all very happy to get back to where they came from."

Thoughts of humans coming from a 'home base' someplace out there add a touch of mystery and excitement to the possibilities life holds. Tauri has never elaborated on the structures and requirements, the purposes and locations, or the entities who make up the group that move from home base back to Earth and maybe back again.

She has said numerous times that there are many, many civilizations who, like themselves, have been monitoring planet Earth for millennia. And, to keep it in proper perspective, she also told us that they monitor many other planets and civilizations as well.

When Lathea tried to dissuade my participation as a channel for the Ogatta group Tauri, visibly upset over the methods employed, said "We never interfere with any of *their* channels!" Dick responded with "I didn't know that they *had* any channels here." "They don't," said Tauri, "but it doesn't matter. They do have them elsewhere."

Dick was unsuccessful in getting the conversation past that statement, but it was very obvious that advanced civilizations monitor other planets and young civilizations in the cosmos. And, because each group has its own method of doing things, it is safe to assume that no two E.T. civilizations employ the same approaches to studying planets and their species.

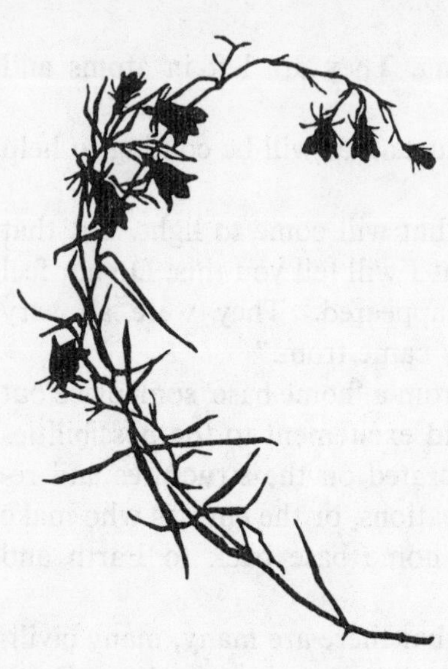

28

YEARS AGO, when I learned to type, I memorized the sentence "Now is the time for all good men to come to the aid of their country." By that time all the memories of my childhood experiences had been wiped out. But now, as I struggle to commit to paper what I know I must, that sentence comes back to me with far more force than it had during my typing exercises. It haunts me as I set down chapter and verse of this story that belongs to every being on this planet.

As I have recounted my experiences, words have often failed me—in most cases because there was no appropriate vocabulary for the phenomenon I wished to describe or explain. But for the scenario that has been given to us, the words are all too clear. They are words that we all know; they describe nature's activities in stark strokes.

"Tell them," I was prodded again and again after my memories were returned, after Dick and I finally said "yes" when the Ogattans asked us to work with them, years later. In Tauri's words:

"You must tell them. Humankind must prepare for what is to

come. Trumpet the voice and scribe the pen. Tell them . . . not just to broaden their horizons and perhaps 'bobble their minds,' but to open their eyes—shake them up, warn them. Tell them so that they will know and you can allay their fears. But tell them first of free will." Predictions are dangerous unless one realizes that free will, human behavior, action and reaction can alter any prediction.

And Tauri has said, "Do you know that if your human beings as one were to change what you call their 'consciousness,' all at once, none of the Scenario would come to pass? But you know and I know that all humanity will not change consciousness simultaneously, in a golden moment, on a slide of light. More is the pity. So the Scenario stands. It is a prediction based on behavior patterns as they exist now. Part of your mission is to tell the people what is to come so that they may be prepared for the changes and not be afraid."

Fear is the static that prevents rational thinking.

Much of the Scenario is already being played out, in precisely the way that catastrophic changes have always been played out all through the long history of the Earth.

A species, human or otherwise, not only lives within its environment but interacts with it. Over a period of time a species can interact so violently that the changes it catalyzes can cause it to change dramatically—even to die out. From the earliest single-cell life form to the human animal, all have interacted with the environment. All have created problems for themselves. All have been the agents of evolutionary change. And all have experienced evolution through cataclysm.

The changes of which the Ogattans speak are brought on, in part, by this interaction. Since the dawning of the scientific age, man has been altering the environment to suit his own needs. One of the leaders of the scientific revolution, Rene Descartes, helped develop a world view based on such a manipulation of the environment. As Fritjof Capra says in *The Turning Point,* "The Cartesian view of the universe as a mechanical system provided a scientific sanction for the manipulation and exploitation of nature that has become typical of Western culture. Descartes shared Sir

Francis Bacon's view that the aim of science was the domination and control of nature."

When single-celled life appeared out of the "soup," three and a half billion years ago, life was very simple. Single cells divided to reproduce. Death as we know it did not exist. But these life forms overpopulated and polluted their environment. Scientists conclude that they reached their "limits to growth." Modification came with the first molecules of chlorophyll. Chlorophyll taught the energy-starved, single-celled world to capture sunlight for food. Photosynthesis was born. But photosynthesis produced a pollutant—oxygen—deadly to the single cells. British scientist James E. Lovelock called oxygen's release the worst atmospheric-pollution incident that this planet has ever known. This cataclysm to the existing species was a major evolutionary event which led to the emergence of multicellular organisms able to handle the poisonous oxygen. And of course, the arrival of oxygen triggered the building of the environment able to support life as we know it.

The multicellular organisms, able to metabolize the deadly oxygen, changed the way many earthly species reproduced. Single-celled organisms were semi-immortal. They reproduced by dividing, lending a continuity to their life. Multicellular organisms were no longer capable of reproducing in this fashion. That is how sexual reproduction entered planet Earth.

That's the good news. The bad news is that the semi-immortality of the single-cell division gave way to the life-and-death cycle of multicellular life.

Charles Darwin published his monumental work on evolution, *On the Origin of Species,* in 1859. But only in the last several years has a workable interpretation surfaced. The brilliant Harvard paleontologist Stephen Jay Gould has shown in his research that species proceed for thousands and millions of years without any sign of evolutionary advancement. Then something happens within their environment—something that either forces a colossal evolutionary leap within a fifty- to one-hundred-year period or causes the species to disappear. In other words, evolution through cataclysm.

Many signs suggest that our current interaction with the environment will force cataclysmic changes in the next two decades.

Our food, for example, is rampant with pesticides—pesticides directly related to the nerve gasses banned from warfare by the Geneva Convention. Their presence in the air we breathe as a byproduct of chemical farming could explain a major portion of the diseases and deformation to which we have fallen victim.

Our onetime abundant water is almost gone. Water, the one thing that neither industries nor farms nor cities can live without, is responding to deforestation and soil erosion by flooding its way to the seas and disappearing. "If you think the oil crisis changed things in this country, wait till the real water crisis hits later this decade," Washington water policy analyst David Weiman has said. A study by the Council of Environmental Quality declares, "In total, about 225 million acres of land in the United States are undergoing severe desertification . . . an area roughly the size of the original 13 states." Americans used approximately 300 billion gallons of water on an average day in 1965. By 1980 that figure had reached 400 billion gallons per day. Current projections show a daily consumption of 900 billion gallons per day by the year 2000.

The water problems of Southern California have been well publicized because this area houses the most productive farmland in the world. Consider that Wyoming, Nebraska, Colorado, New Mexico, Kansas, Oklahoma, Texas, and Arizona face potentially worse water problems than California. The Colorado River has been dammed and drained to a trickle by the time it passes through Arizona. In 1985 the Central Arizona Project diverted greater amounts of the Colorado River water to Tucson and Phoenix to keep them from withering. These desert cities cannot exist without imported water, and demand—even with the increased 1985 allotment—still exceeded supply.

Underlying the seven-state High Plains region is the Ogallala Aquifer, which has been drilled with so many wells that in some areas it is virtually depleted. When this aquifer runs dry, sections of the High Plains states that depend totally on these waters may become desert wastelands.

Elsewhere things are even worse. Intense drought and desertification are spreading in every nation on every continent. Millions of acres of land each year go up in flames, which further wrecks the water system, upsets the ecology, and ruins the land. Soil microorganisms that measured twenty-five tons to the acre of soil at the time of our country's founding today measure about five tons.

In Third World countries unchecked population growth compounds these problems. It leads to increasing political instability, malnutrition, poverty, overgrazing, soil erosion, and deforestation. Demographers say there will be one-third more people by 2000. (I suspect, however, that the very problems caused by nature and man will hold this exploding population to well below the six-billion mark currently projected.)

At a conference in Belgrade, Yugoslavia, with 166 nations participating, trade-and-development authorities reported that in the month they were meeting, June 1983, three and a half million people, half of them children, would die of hunger around the world.

Changing weather patterns are another worrisome factor in the great changes occurring on our planet. According to Fred Ostby, director of the National Severe Storm Center in Kansas City, "One of the things we are seeing is more and more variability [in weather] as time goes by. The longer we keep records, you would think it would get harder and harder to break them, but one of the things that seem a little odd is we seem to be breaking more records. There are wider swings between heat and cold. I'm not sure what it all means. It's wild."

Climatologist Iben Browning confirms these major climate shifts. He writes, "The Toronto 1940 climate will be found in northern Mississippi by 2010. Toledo, Ohio, had an 11-year running average of a 195-day growing season in 1930; now they have a 120-day season. In 1956 the southern portion of Russia, where most of the Soviet grain is grown, had a 100-day growing season. Now, our satellites show snow as late as the middle of June and as early as the middle of August in that area, meaning they have a 60-day growing season for 95-day wheat.

"Although we won't have an ice age, increased volcanic activity will mean that it will get cooler. In fact, from the end of the 1930s (the warmest decade) to the year 2010, the temperature will drop about 2.3 degrees Centigrade, which doesn't sound like much until you realize the crop-growing areas move south about 300 miles per degree-Centigrade drop. It is getting cold again, very fast."

A massive buildup of carbon dioxide in the atmosphere, caused by pollution, not only wreaks havoc with our environment but gravely affects global food production. This carbon dioxide buildup has come about because in Third World countries slash-and-burn economies have devastated vast tracts of woodland. Another major contributing factor is the massive burning of fossil fuels in all countries, especially the industrially developed Western nations.

This buildup is also what is behind the much discussed "greenhouse effect," whose precise consequences authorities disagree about. They do agree, however, that, whatever these consequences prove to be, they will not be happy ones.

In October 1983 the Environmental Protection Agency released a report warning that substantial warming could occur before the end of this century. EPA scientists predicted "catastrophic consequences" if contingency plans were not made rapidly. Some observers complained that even that alert was "too conservative."

A few days later the National Academy of Sciences agreed that the greenhouse effect would mean more than hotter summers and milder winters. A CO_2 buildup could also alter rainfall, affect crop yields, and potentially even melt glaciers, thus causing a dangerous rise in sea level. (Offsetting this dire prediction are studies done by Dr. Reed Bryson of the University of Wisconsin. His data show that historically, when the carbon dioxide content doubled in the atmosphere, nothing of consequence occurred.)

In his book *The Survival of Civilization* John D. Hamaker suggested that the CO_2 buildup, which traps the heat producing infrared radiation in the atmosphere, will not warm the Earth but freeze it, triggering an ice age. In Hamaker's view the buildup of heat at the equator causes large-scale evaporation of ocean waters in the tropics. This warmed air moves to the higher latitudes of the temperate zones and forms a dense cloud-cover. When more moist, warm air from the equator mixes with this cloud, the resulting precipitation is snow, not rain. Glaciers form and spread to cover large temperate-zone land masses.

It seems likely that in the future we will see, more and more, instances of temperature extremes. In every part of the world, records for heat and cold, and rainfall and drought will be set. Offsetting the increases in CO_2 will be cloud coverings mitigating the warming effects and adding to the extremes.

Dick and I became suddenly aware of how this was affecting us personally when, in May 1984, we realized that during the entire past winter we had not been able to complete a single outdoor project that we had carefully scheduled. We had not taken into account the changing weather. We had not noticed the vastly different patterns of freezing and thawing, of torrential downpours and rapid drying. All of this prevented us from making a dent in our land. We knew that none of this weather behavior was really unusual; but the rapid shifts were unprecedented. Our Waynesville neighbors said they had never seen such fickle patterns. All projects stayed on the drawing board, much to our frustration.

The following June, I spent a few days in central Florida, where the temperature in January and February had dipped to sub-zero levels and killed most of the orange and grapefruit trees. The journey south along I-4 from Orlando was like a drive through the graveyard of the citrus industry. Both sides of the road were lined with orchards of dead trees—an eerie and unsettling sight.

The three counties around Reisha Way were not spared either. A thirty-six-hour January chill saw readings dip below the minus-twenties. Many species of plants that had survived happily in the area for more than a century were devastated. All of the boxwoods, all species of holly except those in the wild, many of the hybrid azaleas, and many, many more were wiped out. It will take years and years for the plants to regenerate and grow—and then only if the weather returns to its customary moderation.

"The fact that the greenhouse effect is real is proven," James Hansen, director of NASA's Goddard Institute for Space Studies, states flatly. "It's only a question of magnitude and time."

There is also no question that earthquakes and volcanic activity have risen dramatically in recent years—and the worst is yet to come, make no mistake about that.

In July 1986 the popular-science magazine *Discover* reported, "There is a 50-percent to 90-percent chance that a major quake will devastate Los Angeles in the next fifty years. It could happen in the year 2036. It could happen next week."

In 1985 China had more than twenty quakes measuring 5 or more on the Richter scale. The director of seismology research in that country remarked that "a new period of activity is beginning."

Earthquakes have always been a fact of life throughout the planet, but the major ones, the big quakes, have been sparse, decades apart. No longer. With short time lapses, in growing numbers annually, the big ones—5.5, 6.4, even 8.6 on the Richter scale—are to be seen with increasing regularity.

Volcanoes, newly erupting after hundreds of years of quiet, have become a regular item on the news. Dick and I have flown over Mount St. Helens, over Mexico City, over Kilauea. The great volcanoes Krakotoa and Pelee erupted in the late 1800s. They have not yet been matched. But the incidence of the bigger blasts is growing. The United States has fifty potentially active volcanoes, located in Hawaii, Alaska, Washington, Oregon, and California.

There is another kind of environmental problem. This one affects human beings specifically: stress . . . an almost unbearable kind of stress which underlies our world's proliferating social ills. As the Ogattans pointed out, the human frame evolved at a time when far fewer frequencies of energy played across the planet. Our neurological system must grow and evolve to be able to handle these energies in what will become a "normal" manner.

Said Tauri, "Stress is caused by increases in energies bombarding the human frame."

I sense growing desperation in the many calls, visits, and letters I have received lately. The mounting stresses of life are affecting everyone, whatever his or her age, economic situation, sex, or education. Life is becoming more difficult as the energies playing on our little planet change in preparation for the New Age.

Since 1960 the number of violent crimes in the United States has more than quadrupled. In the 1980s a major crime is committed here every three seconds, a murder every twenty-four minutes. In 1980 23,000 persons were murdered, 650,000 assaulted, 82,000 women raped. "Man's inhumanity to man," says Tauri.

Elsewhere in the world rampant inflation and corruption, and repressive governments are afflicting societies and individuals. In Latin America right-wing death squads torture and kill. In the Soviet Union and Eastern Europe dissenters languish in jail for the crime of speaking freely. Throughout Africa starvation runs rampant and governments, both white and black, war on their own people. "You'd better learn to blur these lines," advises Tauri.

In Europe and the Middle East terrorists from Belfast to Beirut kill cold-bloodedly, hijack airliners and kidnap hostages, often operating as agents of governments (such as Iran, Syria, and Libya) that see such actions as effective means of achieving policy objectives. Authorities warn us that the day may be coming when terrorists are able to subject us to nuclear blackmail, holding whole cities hostage by threatening to blow them up with atomic devices.

Meanwhile the world's supply of nuclear bombs grows alarmingly. Nuclear weapons are no longer a monopoly of the original atomic powers—the United States, the Soviet Union, Great Britain, and France—but now are believed or suspected to be in the hands of Pakistan, India, South Africa, China, Israel, and other countries. The atomic scientists' war clock says we have been fifteen minutes from extinction as a race for the past twenty-five years.

The Chernobyl accident brought the dangers of nuclear technology back to center stage. Over the years and all over the world, as I have spoken about change, people have asked me if nuclear war will be the catastrophic event that will alter the face of the planet. My response has been a consistent no. I foresee no major power's pushing the nuclear button and ushering in nuclear holocaust. Nuclear war does not serve any conceivable national interest of the United States or the Soviet Union. This is why, despite four decades of sometimes intense hostility, the two countries have maintained peace.

I do think, however, that other types of nuclear accidents will occur and these could release deadly radiation. There are 50,000 nuclear devices deployed worldwide in the weapons arsenals of First, Second, and Third World powers. Add to these the 361 electricity-generating nuclear reactors in operation in 1985, with another 144 more to come on-stream before 1995. Were a geological disruption to occur at or near any of the reactors or weapons and cause a breach of the containment vessel, it would create a *de facto* neutron bomb. A neutron bomb is designed to enhance the radiation component at the expense of the thermal fallout and physical blast components. "You'd better be wary of Nature's Plan," cautions the Ogatta group.

Radiation spills of this kind are a clear and present danger. The effects could be enormous, due to the release of a fatal or debilitating dose of highly penetrating prompt radiation.

The Soviet disaster, it should be noted, occurred *without* the aid of an earthquake or other seismic event.

On my desk at the time of the Chernobyl disaster was the April 1986 Worldwatch Paper 69 titled "Decommissioning: Nuclear Power's Missing Link." I had set it aside because the topic frankly didn't look all that interesting. When I read it the night the Russians released news of Chernobyl, I realized how wrong I had been.

"Nuclear plants cannot simply be abandoned at the end of their operating lives or demolished with a wrecking ball," Worldwatch warned. Decommissioning—the process of cleaning up and burying a retired nuclear plant in order to protect the public from radioactivity—is an essential step in the use of nuclear power. Nearly four decades and four hundred power plants into the nuclear age, the question of how to dispose safely and economically of nuclear reactors and their wastes is still largely unanswered. Radioactivity builds up each year the plant operates and all of the contaminated parts and equipment must be securely isolated from people and the environment. Some radioactive elements in plant components will decay quickly but others will remain hazardous for millennia.

Not one of the twenty-six countries with nuclear generating plants is adequately prepared to dismantle a commercial unit. Worldwide there are more than a dozen power reactors already shut down, with another sixty-six likely to retire by the year 2000 and another one hundred sixty-two by 2010. The Humboldt Bay reactor on the northern California coast has been the center of controversy since its retirement in 1976. The unit lies in a seismologically active zone and is not built to withstand earthquakes—which is why it was permanently taken out of operation. Immediate dismantlement would safeguard the public against potential exposure to radiation. Yet efforts to dismantle this plant are not expected until after 2000.

Elsewhere in the United States five reactors used to make plutonium for atomic bombs have no containment features at all. Forty-nine nuclear power plants have containment structures less capable than Chernobyl's of withstanding the force of a hydrogen explosion. Nuclear Regulatory Commission member James Asseltine says an accident at an American reactor could release comparable levels of radiation: "Our reactors were not designed for large-scale core-melt accidents." He said that, unless further steps are taken, "we can expect to see a core-melt accident in the next twenty years and possibly a radiation release equal to or greater than the one at Chernobyl."

Discussions about decommissioning typically exclude the topic of high-level nuclear waste disposal. But high-level wastes must be removed from the plant before decommissioning can proceed. At present not a single country has a permanent disposal facility for high-level wastes and no such facilities are likely to be in operation before the turn of the century.

In the United States virtually all of the twelve thousand metric tons of spent fuel produced to date is now stored temporarily in water-filled utility holding ponds. The volume of waste is expected to quadruple within fifteen years! Utilities do not have adequate space for storing this spent fuel, nor is there any place they can send it.

According to Worldwatch, "Health risks can only be avoided by keeping wastes out of the biosphere until they have decayed to harmless levels. On most contaminated parts radioactivity declines more than twentyfold during the first thirty years of storage. But the toxicity of high-level wastes requires that they be kept out of the biosphere for tens of thousands of years—longer than recorded history. Since reliance on human institutions for such a long period of time is impossible, most countries have decided to bury their wastes in geological repositories 300 to 1200 meters below the Earth's surface. Searching for stable sites is the current focus of most disposal programs."

We have opened a nuclear Pandora's box.

There was an earlier tragic nuclear accident, officially hushed up by the host country. A British newspaper gave this account in 1986:

"Carelessly stored heat-generating nuclear waste was the cause of the world's worst nuclear holocaust, the radiation from which is still self-boiling and seeping to you, wherever you may be. It happened in 1958–59 at Kyshtym. An area larger than Southern England was devastated and two hundred thousand Russians contaminated. Thousands of slave laborers were fatally irradiated as they bulldozed six towns and asphalted them over in a vain effort to contain the nuclear activity released. The area is still uninhabitable."

The London *Times* for April 29, 1986, refers to Kyshtym and to "six villages being devastated and their names being deleted from Soviet atlas references." Two of these villages had populations of 30,000, three had 38,000, and the largest had over 80,000 inhabitants.

Meanwhile, as this terrible nuclear danger hangs over our heads, so-called "conventional wars" rage (forty-four wars and revolutions going on at this writing). Thirty children die every minute for want of food and inexpensive vaccines, while the world's military spends $1.3 million on weapons that same minute.

We have been speaking of change since the mid-seventies when the Ogatta group entered our lives. It has been a repetitive and more urgent drumbeat as the years have passed. Some hear it and are moving steadily toward a course of planned survival. Others who have listened to the message over many years suspect us of "crying 'wolf!'" After all, the stock market averages have reached all-time highs and "big bucks" have been made; "What's so terrible?"

Futurist Robert Theobold says, "Changes can only occur when the breakdown of the old becomes truly obvious and the vision of the new becomes clear." Neither is the case now. But when the problems and their solutions become clear to all, will it be too late to accumulate the necessities for survival?

The world population is projected by demographers to pass the six billion mark by the turn of the century. Knowledgeable leaders and futurists in such diverse fields as religion, climatology, and parapsychology predict less than two billion will see the beginning of the twenty-first century. We hope they are very wrong! But if indeed "billions of people will not make it" through the changes, we can't help pondering what will emerge as the major cause of such alarming and catastrophic numbers departing this planet. Is it possible, as in times long past—in biblical times—that the potential killer catastrophe will be a plague? Is it conceivable that an AIDS, for example, could wipe out a major portion of the world's population?

We don't know. No one knows. Don't let anyone tell you that he knows. But think of the awesome possibilities.

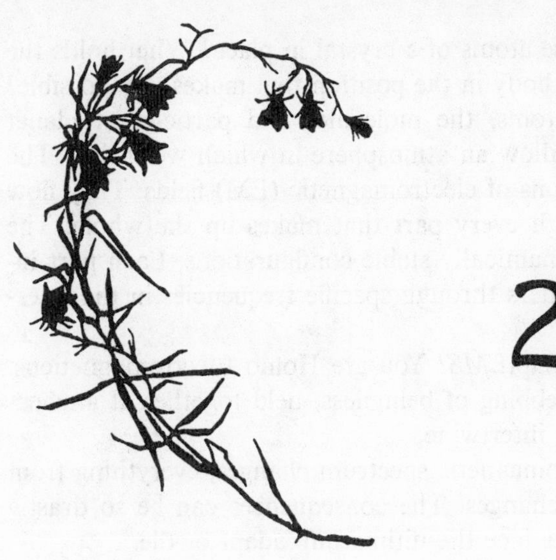

29

WHAT CAUSES the havoc and the violence that we find within and around us? The explanation begins with the fact that man is an electrical being; an electromagnetic system matriculating in an EM environment. This theory has been developing for over a hundred and fifty years, ever since Dubois-Raymond proved that the nerve force is electrical. Only in the last decade, however, have we begun to understand that from the tiniest atom in your body, to your brain and your aura, you are a creature of electromagnetic interactions—and so is our planet, the solar system, and our universe.

You probably know that comparatively speaking, the atoms in a crystal are as far from each other as the planets in the solar system are from themselves and the sun. You also know that you, along with every object around you, are mostly empty space. Arthur Koestler wisely said, "The chair on which you sit seems a hard fact, but I know that you sit on a nearly empty vacuum. This room, with a few specks of dust floating in the air, is overcrowded . . . compared to the molecular emptiness which you call a chair and on which your fundamentals rest."

What holds these atoms of a crystal in place? What holds the atoms within your body in the position that makes you possible? What holds the atoms, the molecules and particles of planet Earth in place to allow an atmosphere in which we thrive? The answer is interactions of electromagnetic (EM) fields. They flow around and through every part that makes up the whole. The EM fields form dynamically stable configurations. Each part interacts with the others through specific frequencies in the interweaving fields.

You are Homo Sapi*EMS!* You are Homo Electromagneticus. You are a spiderwebbing of beingness, held together at anchor-points where fields intertwine.

When the electromagnetic spectrum changes, everything from you to the Earth changes. The consequences can be so drastic that we as a species face the ultimatum: adapt or die.

These changes started when Man began to harness and use the electromagnetic spectrum. We have gone from evolving in a basically simple spectrum with hardly any EM waves in it, to a complex environment filled with EM radiation. All man-made radiation is *abnormal.* It never existed before on Earth. And it does have bio-effects. No one considered the possibility that one day the magnetic ripples from our technical advances would affect our well-being.

The first effects came after Nikola Tesla developed the multiphase generator. It allowed electricity to be transported long distances in an alternating-current (AC) form. In this country the AC used was sixty cycles per second, a stimulating frequency. By the time the nation was wired from coast to coast, that stimulation was affecting almost everyone. The stimulation multiplied with the maturing of industry and the rapid growth of new technologies. But human beings could accommodate these frequencies. The sixty-cycle frequency was said to have a positive effect: it increased human intelligence, creativity, and achievement.

Even radio's long, looping, modulated energy waves had no negative effect. But the high, short radar and TV frequencies were something else again.

A frequency is a stream of waves of energy, of packets of energy. The low frequencies are long, looping waves. The high frequencies are tiny, millionths of an inch long. They are "invisible," high in energy, and able to go through a building, a body, an object, the Earth. Radar and high-frequency TV come in energy packets high in the spectrum. They come in packets of energy each small enough to be contained within a nerve cell, giving the cells an electrical signal that has no meaning to the cells but to which they try to respond.

Much of the electromagnetic stimulation we receive today keeps our adrenals pumping. This stimulation we call *stress.* Research in the new field of psychoneuroimmunology has shown that when the endocrine system is primed, pumping adrenalin, the immune system is depressed. In plain language, *stress* stops the normal working of our immune defense system and allows immunofailure diseases such as cancer, arthritis, and many others to flourish.

The first generations subjected to radar and TV bombardment responded with nervous fatigue and other physical ailments. But the new generation coming on—conceived, born, and bred in the new high frequencies—seems to have expanded its abilities to handle the problem. More and more people are developing the ability to "dance to the new tunes."

One result is that many have developed new abilities: telepathy, psychokinesis, psychometry, the manipulation of atomic fields so that, for example, spoons can be bent—or, as in an experience I had, rocks can be broken with the hands. I had the advantage of learning the "art" from the Ogattans.

One day a young man named Michael, a special student of mine for well over a decade, was visiting me. I had introduced him to yoga, to reflex balance, and to the use of *rooting* as it applies to healing (the concept of energy's being drawn up from the living ball of matter we call Earth). I taught Michael to see auras; afterward he began to emerge from the totally physical world of karate (he is a sixth-degree Black Belt and First Level Grand Master in Tai Chi Chuan-Kempo), and to move toward a synthesis of mental and physical activity. In teaching this exceptional student, I had developed surges of energy which I never knew existed.

Earlier in the course of instruction an entity named Master Ching had assumed the channel, drawing me out of the body and taking complete control. That first time, Ching assumed a very low "fight stance"; with his (my) knees almost touching the ground, he began to circle around Michael. He demonstrated pressure-point techniques and survival kata which Michael said were so incredibly fast, advanced, and graceful that the "fighting" we did was no contest.

I hadn't a chance against Ching either! My body was one royal mess after he took over my vehicle. I learned to live with muscle cramps and charley horses, cheerfully putting up with them. Ching taught Michael an art of which I knew absolutely nothing.

On the day in question Ching had suggested to Michael that he learn how to break boards and rocks with an open hand. Ching said Michael should get in tune with the rock, then go out and split one bare-handed. When I say "said," I mean that Ching, who did not speak when in the channel, indicated his desire through gesture. Ching never spoke; his intentions were usually clear. When they were not, Tauri came through to explain. She had come through after our first meeting with Ching, to tell us his name and a bit of his history.

At any rate, after this suggestion had been made, Ching left the channel and Michael told me about Ching's idea. The two of us went outside and selected a huge rock, one we could barely lift. After some deep breathing Michael slowly lifted his hand. I counted to three and he let his hand drop to the rock in a soft-break technique. The rock remained intact but Mike's hand began to swell. He tried it again with the same result.

Suddenly I was inspired to suggest that I stand behind Mike and summon up the Earth's energy. I would put my hand lightly on top of his. We would then drop our hands together on the rock. Mike and I did some preparatory deep breathing. After the one-two-three count, we dropped our hands, mine over his, onto the rock. Although we touched it with little or no force, the rock split wide open and fell into two pieces.

I realized that for the rock to split as it did we had to have disturbed part of the rock's EM pattern. What had happened? I believe that Michael and I had drawn some Earth energy and imparted it to the rock. We energized the atoms and molecules at the point of our focus and caused them to "speed up." The change in the atoms' pulsing broke the integrity of the rock's EM field. This change allowed the rock to break when Michael's hand gently struck it.

We are in a new time. Additional sensory awareness is developing under the stimulation of the broadened spectrum of frequencies with which we are being bombarded. Today many children come into the world "native to the New Age." Dr. Ibarra Chavez, a leading pediatrician in Mexico City, told me that the new crop of babies is amazing: more alert and aware, eyes focussed and necks stronger. "The differences we note in the babies over the last decade," Dr. Chavez said, "are incredible!"

He specializes in premature infants. He said, "These tiny infants no bigger than chickens lie in their bassinets, and with their heads up they are looking around the nursery!" I wonder if a new species is indeed awakening to a cosmic calling.

A higher form of life should be spawned because it is needed.

The Ogattans ascribe great importance to the role of parenting. They say that our children will be the great hope of our own future. The children are bred to the New Age and will be able to handle the changes. We must give them the love, the understanding, the knowledge, and the freedom to meet change on its own terms.

Tauri has said, "Don't minimize the vibrations . . . that are bombarding this piece of the cosmos. The little ones are more able to handle them than you can possibly know. The question is the elders . . ."

Yet everyone, young or old, is being affected. In the January/February 1987 issue of *American Health,* Reverend Andrew Greeley, a Roman Catholic priest who, in addition to being a bestselling novelist, is also a sociologist, reports the results of a survey conducted at the University of Chicago's National Opinion Research Council (NORC). The study revealed that "two thirds of all adults (67 percent) now report having experienced ESP. In 1973, it was 58 percent in a similar poll."

Dr. Greeley says that 5 percent of American adults report feeling (in the words of one) "very close to a powerful, spiritual force that seemed to lift you out of yourself." "These experiences go way beyond intellect, and even beyond emotion," Greeley writes. "What was paranormal is now normal. It's even happening to elite scientists and physicians who insist that such things cannot possibly happen. Indeed, the nation is living with a split between scientific belief and personal reality."

Greeley reports that the NORC poll showed that people who have such experiences are not nuts but "ordinary Americans, somewhat above the norm in education and intelligence." Such experiences "are common, benign and, often helpful . . . They could even change the nature of our society."

But what of the changes that affect the planet itself? We can see their effects in the proliferation of "natural catastrophes." Planet Earth is responding to something, just as we, with our wars, terrorism, stress, and fear, are responding to something.

In part the planet is responding to changes we have made with our atomic tests and our radar and TV broadcasts. In part she is responding to the physical changes caused by our deforestations and pollutions. In turn, we are starting to respond to man-made changes in our planet's ecosphere.

What will come of all this? Will Mother Earth shake herself free of the forces that are creating such havoc? Will she keep us from destroying her along with ourselves?

The Ogattans say "Yes!" They tell us that she will remineralize the soil through volcanic action that will bring the minerals from beneath the crust and scatter them across her face. They say she will rearrange her continental plates into more comfortable positions. Her face will be altered in a new and less stressful pattern, all before the turn of the century.

The Ogattans say there is a new, expanded, more intelligent way of life on the far side of the cataclysm. A better civilization is waiting to be born in "a Golden Tomorrow."

People are always telling Dick and me that they do not want to bring children into this troubled world. "Get married! Have babies!" I tell them. Dick and I have rejoiced in the birth of our first two grandchild. "Button," Tauri dubbed the first boy, Michael, and, "a valentine," she said of Alex, his tiny brother, twenty-one months later. Our "architects of the future," two of the new breed that will help the Earth find its cosmic destiny. Those children will face a newer and more exciting future than any we have dreamed. We fantasize about more grandchildren yet to come. (At this writing, one is due any day.)

It is the children who represent the future of our civilization. We sometimes lose sight of this. We relegate their educators to the bottom of the economic heap and discourage many would-be educators from realizing their rightful contribution.

The basic unit of strength that supports their growth, the two-parent home, has undergone a dramatic change as the divorce rate has climbed these last decades. It takes two parents working in harmony to provide an environment of support that a child needs to maximize his potential.

In the Ogatta jorpah, child-raising is held to be so important that the parental unit consists of five individuals, not two. They work together to maximize the growth and potential of each new being. The unit consists of three females and two males, and each brings to the task various skills and perspectives. In this environment the youth is able to call on many strengths and manners of support during his formative years.

In addition, the unit of five allows the adult members to continue their professions or vocations without interruption. There are always other members available for the parenting problems if one should be taken away from the home on a work-oriented project. This is a current problem in our own society as both parents, more often than not, are called upon to work and make a financial contribution to the nest. These are problems we will have to solve as we go forward into the New Age.

When precisely will the great changes come?

For many centuries prophets have spoken of a coming Great Purification. This sense of an impending cataclysm and rebirth was shared by Aztecs, Hopis, Tibetans, American Indians, Nostradamus, and numerous others in all times and places.

In our own time Edgar Cayce, the celebrated "sleeping prophet," said that one sign that will herald the violent transition period into a more viable life for mankind will be the rising of Atlantis. He did not say that Atlantis will rise again, although he did speak of land masses rising and falling. Is the "Atlantis" to which he refers our space vehicle *Atlantis?*

The Chippewa Bear tribe have a tradition that says purification will come "after the whites have built a house in the sky." The space-lab we are now building?

These prophecies refer to specific events but not to specific times. Perhaps it is not possible for prophets to set an exact date (indeed, the record of a long list of failed end-of-the-world prophecies strongly attests to that), but perhaps a good general estimate can be made, using both reason and intuition. According to our friend Dr. Puharich, both the Mayan and Egyptian calendars ended August 15, 1986, and marked the beginning of the "hell period" for our civilization. The Aztec calendar ceases at August 15, 1987. What does all of this mean? I suspect that we are facing the changes within the next couple of decades, with major changes as early as 1988.

It takes no profound insight to see that our planet is already changing. The changes are on an exponential curve and we have entered the swift upswing of that curve. As I noted earlier, Dick and I have watched the hurricanes, the tornadoes, the vicious snowstorms that have shattered records in the Northwest; we have seen floods all over the world, and marked the devastation from desertification and fire. We have compared what we have observed with the information sent to us from around the world. In effect, we have been timing Mother Earth's labor pains.

We have drawn into our ken experts from around the world. We have listened. We have invited to our home the most knowledgeable authorities on subjects that relate to our needs. They have shared their expertise with us.

From all of this, from the knowledge of many, Dick and I with the help of of our extraterrestrial friends have come to these conclusions:

Violent planetary changes will occur within the two decades of the 1980s and 1990s, making life radically different for those who survive it. We who have seen it coming must do all in our power to make that new life better than the life before it.

We will have the assistance, though not the interference, of extraterrestrials who will serve as midwives to this rebirth into a happier future.

It is entirely up to us to decide whether we will equip ourselves with the abilities and knowledge needed to come to grips with that future.

Over the millennia human beings have proven themselves to be survivors. The tools for survival are in our hands. And the first priority is to have a goal.

Why do you want to survive? Many don't. They say simply, "If it's going to be like that, I'd rather just go out with the majority. I don't want to live through it."

Why survive? It won't be easy. It won't be pretty. It will be about as rough as anything can get.

When a whole civilization is turned upside down by the factors it has helped to create, when Mother Nature seems to become an enemy instead of a friend, when people are perishing across the face of this globe, why survive? Why accept the challenge inherent in that awful law of nature: adapt or disappear?

Speaking for Dick and me—and no one can speak for other than himself—I will say we find the future that we face a challenge such as nothing else could possibly offer. What can be more challenging than building from the bottom up? We hope to be part of it. We want to be part of it. We will do everything possible to make ourselves part of it. When else could we have found a possibility so great, so difficult and demanding a task, so rewarding a future if we are successful?

We know that it will call on every resource that we as human beings have developed over many centuries. We know it will entail the greatest demands imposed on the species in the last few million years. We know that we will be depending on the greatest abilities we can produce, to see us through to a new world, to a golden tomorrow.

Then there is the great potential on the far side of the catastrophe. There is the new life beginning. Our civilization, which has made monumental mistakes, is worth rebuilding. It can meet its highest potentials. On the other side of those cataclysms man will truly reach for—and reach—the stars. Man will prove himself worthy of the evolutionary process that has gone into his making.

We want to be part of that restructuring. We want to have a hand in building something new and finer, taking advantage of the best of the old in order to create the new.

That is our goal. That is the why of our planning, changing, and working. We want to be in a position to survive, and to herald the changes. We want to be able to provide a network of information for those who will hear and who have the same goal.

Before you do anything else, you must find out if and why you want to see it through to the other side. Otherwise there is no reason whatsoever to make all the concessions and put in all the effort necessary to prepare.

The second most important thing you must do is to think rationally. It may not seem rational, in these closing years of the twentieth century, to expect to be put up against changes that spell the end of almost everything we have known, and to prepare for such a conclusion. Yet is it more rational to ignore what is so very plainly written in the events of today?

Train yourself to think in terms of solutions. Teach yourself to look for, and find, answers to the many questions. They may not be ideal solutions—but any decision is better than none. Nobody but you expects you to be perfect. Grant yourself the right to do the best you can. The main thing is to put your best answers into motion. And always maintain confidence in yourself, in your ability to do the right things in the best way you know how.

For years, members of the Mormon church have been instructed to keep one or two years' supply of foodstuffs, clothing, tools—all the essentials for survival—in places where those things would be most useful come catastrophe. Other groups, less well-known, are doing the same. We have drawn from their expertise in our own storage and survival posture.

Once you have decided your goals, how will you proceed?

Are you willing to relocate, now? Or, if not that, to establish a remote hideaway where you can go for short periods of time now and for the eventual long haul?

We know three couples, none of whom could have afforded a hideaway themselves, who have bought land and built and stocked a place together. It will serve as a vacation spot for all in the interim, and as a refuge when the need arises.

Dick and I are often asked why we chose to live in the western mountains of North Carolina. "Did the Ogatta group direct you there?" people want to know.

Well, yes and no. The Ogattans said to find a place, and they provided us with suggestions concerning its character. But it was we who found the spot. We do not think of it as *the* definitive place to be, the only safe place. If this were so, we wouldn't have moved there because of the hoards that would also be there. There are thousands of safe places, not just one, and be wary of *anyone* who tells you anything to the contrary. No one knows for certain; but there are sensible guidelines we can look to for our own confirmations.

We moved to this area for many reasons, not the least of which is the beauty and the peacefulness of the place and its surroundings. It has numerous advantages. All water emanates from within the county; there is none flowing into it. There are numerous springs right on our property. There is a substantial quartz (not limestone) content in the mountains that surround us. This provides a very high energy level.

"What shall I look for?" people ask. I would not presume to tell another how or where to live, but Dick and I can pass along some of our own guidelines which helped us determine where to relocate. Ask yourself these questions:

1. Is the location you have in mind far enough from a major city to be safe in case of strikes, shortages, rioting? Stress is al-

ready creating violent conditions far in advance of the complete changes.

2. Is it within reasonable distance of an airport? There will be living time between now and then. This is for travel purposes, company, and freight and express mails.

3. What are the cultural resources within a radius of one hundred miles? Neighbors accustomed to culture make good survival neighbors.

4. How are the shifting weather patterns affecting the area?

5. How close is it to a fault line? A nuclear facility? A pollution-producing industry?

6. What is the independence level of the average citizen?

7. Has the crime rate dropped or risen in recent years?

8. Can you grow your own food for year-round storage?

9. Are you permanently tied to your life-style? Job? Geography? Think about these honestly and carefully.

10. What is the water situation?

"Surviving" is a term applicable to everyday living, not just during and after catastrophe. People seek change, then often resist it. We did not. We sought beauty in the meantime and survival in the long run. We have learned from our experience at Reisha Way that a retreat can be a pleasure, before, during and—we assume—after.

Once you are there—or once you have found an alternative spot to the possibly dangerous one in which you normally live—or even if you have just located a spot in the woods where you can practice camping until a time comes when you need to camp and build for survival—what are the things you need to have available?

There are innumerable places where you can get information on the types of foodstuffs and clothes that can be stored and kept ready and waiting. We list a number of them regularly in the *Woodrew Update,* the newsletter we send out bimonthly. This sort of information you need to obtain and study.

We can, however, emphasize two things:

Water is the limiting factor. It is the one thing you can do without for only the shortest period of time. Be sure your source of water is not dependent on electricity or on any of the forces of today's civilization. City water, even in the smallest cities, is normally dependent on pumping, and pumping is dependent on electricity.

Store what you eat, and eat what you store. Organize your thoughts and take time to research what you really use and what you just think you need.

For four weeks keep a list of daily menus and all items used in preparing them. You will have a realistic picture of what your family consumes; by multiplying by twelve, you can store realistically for a year.

If you are able to relocate, storage space must be a major consideration. That is also true, of course, of a retreat spot. If you must simply depend on a camping spot, storage will be a problem, but not an insoluble one if you put your mind to it. And in your current home or apartment, don't overlook the storage space available under your bed or behind your couch.

"What will happen?" "When will it happen?" "How will it happen?" "Where should I go?"

These kinds of requests for specifics bombard us at S.T.A.R. headquarters. These are questions we cannot—and would not try to—answer. As Tauri has said, that sort of information abridges the free will of those who ask for specifics.

"Let me know before a major quake hits Tokyo because my mother lives there." "Tell me when Mount Shasta or Mount St. Helens or any of the others will erupt again because we are planning to build a summer home in the area." "Is it safe for me to take a trip to the east or west, north or south in the month of April, June, November?" "Where is the safest place to build a retreat?"

It is pointless to ask for answers to these questions from anyone except yourself. "When and where will the terrorists strike next?" "Will there be riots in my area?" To persons who ask "readings" from me, I say simply, "Please do not look outside yourself for the answers. Look within. No teacher on this or any other plane can know the truth for you. You are the only person who can create your own reality." I do not do "readings" for my children, my husband, or myself. I would never consider it for others. The important point is that you should never let *anyone* tell you what to do, or that his way is the only way, whether he is a psychic, a channel, an astrologer, or a would-be guru.

Inherent in the ability to survive is the ability to make your own decisions based on your own knowledge and according to your own rules and timetables. You know what your situation is. And, above all, you know whether the game is worth the candle to you personally and to those you love.

The Ogatta group has emphasized from the beginning that it will point directions. It will never, never give directives. This is an attitude that allows us to work with them. We respect and seek to emulate this method when Dick and I scribe the pen or trumpet the voice.

If you think your home base is in a threatened locale, you should devise alternate plans. Think of the second area as an insurance policy.

If you are in a town ripe for strikes, riots, nuclear waste leaks, water or food shortages, then prepare, as we are preparing, for those possibilities. Feel good about your preparations.

No, I can't tell you when, where, why, or how. Neither can anyone else! I can only tell you that between now and the turn of the century major changes will occur on this planet and they will alter your way of life. Depend on it.

Something else you can depend on, absolutely, is this: Should widespread disaster begin to occur, each level of government will most likely elect to institute its disaster-and-evacuation plan. These plans are instruments by which governments arm themselves with emergency powers to use in times of disaster. Their purpose is to limit the scope of the catastrophe. They include cordoning off the area so that no one can get in and no one can get out. Military and paramilitary forces are used to impose martial law upon the area, should they deem it necessary.

If disaster is widespread and severe, the state border can be sealed immediately and no one will be allowed to come in or go out unless he is part of the martial plan. Travel on highways will be restricted and directed exactly according to the dictates of those in charge. Your freedom of movement can be severely, even violently, restricted.

After a major disaster, those stricken will not have much to say or do about anything, unless they have devised methods to meet the situations that can be so clearly foreseen. Methods for getting to where you need to go must be part of your plans now. And as you make these plans, you must remember that you will not be the only ones fleeing.

It would be well to remember some sobering facts about America's infrastructure. Not long before we left Connecticut to move to the Great Smoky Mountains, a one-hundred-foot section of a bridge over which we had commuted for more than thirty years getting to New York City collapsed. It was a bridge on the Connecticut Turnpike. A minor tragedy in comparison to others since. Nonetheless it called attention to the fact that America's infrastructure is crumbling; and in any disaster such crumbling is likely to be a contributor to chaos.

A year before, *Newsweek* had reported that "a vision of urban apocalypse is not farfetched." Roads, bridges, sewers, rails, and mass-transit systems are collapsing. The Connecticut Turnpike bridge collapse was less a freak incident than we would like to think. Think about all those bridges you drive over every day, the subways you ride, the tunnels you go through; you would have to use these if you were fleeing. What would you do if their use were restricted to you?

Do you think that in time of emergency you could go to the bank and withdraw your savings? That your credit cards would be honored? To get to where you will need to be, you will need gasoline, perhaps a tire, perhaps a battery. Do you think that the man who pumps your gasoline will remain calmly waiting to serve you at his station? Or that, if electricity is gone, he would be able to pump gasoline if he did wait?

Another important fact: People best suited for survival are those who are open to new ideas and new ways of doing.

We are the fortunate. It is the New Age people who join the S.T.A.R. Foundation, become visitors to the S.T.A.R. House, subscribe to our newsletter, and make themselves part of our lives. Many listen to our message of change and do something about it. There is no right way or wrong way of preparation—just the way you determine to do it for yourself and for your family. No two life-styles or mode of living are the same. We have had S.T.A.R. supporters take our message and run with their own ball in directions utterly foreign to our way of thinking. And that's fine. There are many roads to the top of the mountain.

We find it both stimulating and rewarding, having agreed to "trumpet the voice and scribe the pen," to encourage people to take the steps that will lead to a better future for mankind, to be central to those who are taking the steps and finding solutions. We have found, moreover, that, in moving ourselves and our lives into an environment that is uplifting in and of itself, we are the beneficiaries. We find that our abilities, our awareness, and our consciousness are expanding.

Here I can again hear the colors, see the music. We can increase our abilities as the structures imposed by a deteriorating civilization are removed from us. We can now come alive from our toes to the top of our heads. We can interact with an environment that speaks of growth and fulfillment. There is no danger we will face that can destroy the happiness that we have found here.

I have a very strong message for you. Now is the time to make important decisions for yourself and your family. The decisions concern preparing for change. Nobody can make them for you. In our family we say that there are no bad decisions, only bad results—in which case you make another decision. What is the best way to proceed?

This morning when I got dressed, I reached for a favorite whimsical art form of jewelry. It is a pendant made up of all kinds of pieces of old but lovely watches which no longer work: hands, springs, dials, wheels, faces. As I hung it around my neck, it occurred to me that it was indeed a very "timely" piece. Time is something we are running out of. Clocks are slowing down—or speeding up—depending on the way one handles things as they are, each in his or her own way. Life as we have always known it is in transition and about to change radically.

Examine the thesis of *change* in a "think and relate" way. Dick and I have been broadcasting this message for better than a decade. We are no longer labeled "apostles of doom and gloom." Our message, our scenario of change, is now part of the front-page headlines in every newspaper and magazine around the world. It is the way things *are.* And the way things are is exactly what we envisioned they would be more than a decade ago. The tempo is increasing, as the E.T.s predicted. "Right on target."

In our opinion current news and scientific discoveries corroborate the changes our Ogattan friends have long been outlining for us. Everything points to major changes in the near future.

If in your view we are wrong in this, your decision to continue your current way of living without making preparations is warranted. But do yourself a favor—examine the evidence carefully. Don't back into inaction because it's the easy way. If you choose not to act, do so because you are convinced that we are mistaken and that all will be well (and know that we hope you're right). If, however, you agree with the message of change, then *now* is the time to prepare.

When the Ogatta group rolled the Destiny Screen, I learned that Mother Nature is no mother; she is a tyrant. She is prone to fits and starts of violence: hurricanes, floods, super-magnetic storms, droughts, earthquakes, volcanoes, famines, plagues, tidal waves. The very look of the Earth will shift.

The Ogatta group has invested a great deal of time and energy in my training so that I could forewarn you that this scenario will come to pass in our lifetime. In linking communications with advanced, benign civilizations, human beings will progress up the evolutionary ladder. We will be the beneficiaries of new technologies, new means of communication, and new ways of handling our new existence. And after the many changes there will follow a brighter tomorrow, although a very different one, for future generations of human beings. We must have all our wits about us if we are to survive.

After you have read this book and stretched your awareness, I hope we can welcome you among our S.T.A.R. supporters and hence our "extended family." Together we can look upward to the cosmos, downward to changes in the Earth's core, backward to bits of age-old wisdom that are applicable to our current situation, and forward to glimpses of the future provided by our extraterrestrial friends and mentors. All participation is welcome because it is about—and for—all of us.

To receive the *Woodrew Update* you need only support S.T.A.R.'s work. A tax-deductible donation of *$30 or more (U.S.A.), $35 or mor*[illegible] *more outside the U.S.A./Canada t*[illegible]it Skin Road, Waynesville, N[illegible]ings you the Updates, and[illegible]s held at the S.T.A.R. Hou[illegible]tunity to share your thoughts a[illegible]aphically diverse but like-minded wonderful group of people. (Autographed books are also available through S.T.A.R.)

The countdown to tomorrow is well underway. It is no longer in the distant future. We will look back to this period in the late eighties and recognize the dramatic changes taking place.

My Destiny Screen is clear. Dick and I changed our lives in anticipation of the coming Scenario. A decade ago, when I stepped outside the structure and lectured to business groups on the coming changes, I had a great deal to lose and nothing to gain. With twenty/twenty hindsight, I realize that—in truth—I gained a great deal and lost nothing. We love it here in the mountains. We have been able to help many in all age brackets consider awesome possibilities, embrace new concepts, expand their consciousness and develop their psi abilities. Healing sessions bring joy to us and wholeness to the participants.

The S.T.A.R. House has turned into a University of the Future. We chart paths through the coming transitions into the Golden Tomorrow. Our research and messages in the *Woodrew Update* newsletters are written as "think and relate" pieces. We have become a unique family, a part of the changing Universe. Nature's catastrophies lie ahead, and the challenges of a new and better civilization are on the far side.

The children are grown, married, and very much a solid support system. One is building a house on the mountain to be more closely involved with our work. The others will come when the time is right. Meanwhile, we encourage each other on the phone and through the mail. Friends from Connecticut visit and marvel at the serene quality of life we enjoy as we prepare for what lies ahead. And prepare we must, so prepare we do.

What if we are wrong? We hope we *are* wrong. We say it and we mean it. *"If all humanity changed its consciousness in one golden moment, then none of the Scenario would come to pass,"* said Tauri. *"But you know and I know that they will not. And so the Scenario stands."*

So I scribe the pen as we listen for distant rumbles. And as the volcano makes its thunder on a clear day in preparation to erupt, so too will we provide our "thunder." Our hope is that you who choose to listen will do what you must to insure your secure position. *"Architects of the future,"* the Ogatta group calls tomorrow's leaders. Leaders of all ages and skills and from all walks of life will be needed. We hope that you are among them. We hope you will think and relate to the clarion call of my *Memories of Tomorrow.*

ABOUT THE AUTHOR

Greta Woodrew classifies herself as a futurist. She is the author of one other book, *On a Slide of Light.* She also serves as vice president of Space Technology and Research Foundation (S.T.A.R.), which advances all aspects of psychic phenomena and psi research.